Texas Assessment Preparation

Preparation

Grade 11

HOLT McDOUGAL

Literature

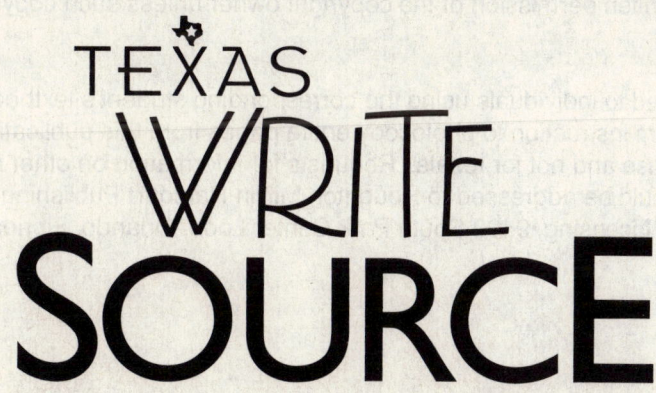

TEXAS

WRITE

SOURCE

 HOUGHTON MIFFLIN HARCOURT

Contents

How to Use This Book vi

PART I: PREPARING FOR TEXAS ASSESSMENTS

Guided Reading

Reading Literary Text: Fiction 4
 "The Mentor" 5

Reading Literary Text: Literary Nonfiction 12
 from "Presidential Address on the Declaration of War on Japan" 13

Reading Literary Text: Poetry 21
 "A Bird Came Down the Walk" 22

Reading Literary Text: Drama 27
 Something's Changed 28

Reading Informational Text: Expository Text 37
 from *My First Summer in the Sierra* 38

Reading Informational Text: Persuasive Text 44
 "School Newspapers Should Be Uncensored" 45

Reading Informational Text: Paired Selections 52
 "The Pleasure of Books" 54
 "The Future of the Book: Printed or Electronic?" 56

Reading Practice

Literary Text: Fiction
 "Ginger for the Heart" 68

Literary Text: Literary Nonfiction
 "Leaving Home" 75

Literary Text: Poetry
 "After Apple-Picking" 80

Literary Text: Drama
 from "In the Fog" 84

Informational Text: Expository Text
 "9/11 Dogs Seemed to Escape Illnesses" 91

Informational Text: Persuasive Text
 "Good Parents Don't Allow Teens to Circumnavigate" 96

Informational Text: Paired Selections
 from "Appearances Are Destructive" 102
 from "Manual on School Uniforms" 104

Written Composition

Persuasive Essay 1 113
    Benchmark Composition and Rubric: Score Point 4 114
    Benchmark Composition and Rubric: Score Point 2 116
Persuasive Essay 2 119
    Benchmark Composition and Rubric: Score Point 4 120
    Benchmark Composition and Rubric: Score Point 2 122
Analytical Essay 1 125
    Benchmark Composition and Rubric: Score Point 4 126
    Benchmark Composition and Rubric: Score Point 2 128
Analytical Essay 2 131
    Benchmark Composition and Rubric: Score Point 4 132
    Benchmark Composition and Rubric: Score Point 2 134
Written Composition Practice: Persuasive Essay 1 136
Written Composition Practice: Persuasive Essay 2 137
Written Composition Practice: Analytical Essay 1 138
Written Composition Practice: Analytical Essay 2 139

Revising and Editing

Guided Revising 142
Revising Practice 1 145
Revising Practice 2 147
Guided Editing 149
Editing Practice 1 152
Editing Practice 2 154

PART II: *TEXAS WRITE SOURCE* ASSESSMENTS

Pretest 158
Progress Test 1 168
Progress Test 2 178
Post-test 188

Contents

How to Use This Book

Texas Assessment Preparation contains instruction that will help you develop the reading and writing skills tested on the State of Texas Assessments of Academic Readiness (STAAR). In addition, this book includes tests that accompany the Houghton Mifflin Harcourt *Texas Write Source* program.

PART I: PREPARING FOR TEXAS ASSESSMENTS

Part I of the book will help you develop skills assessed on the STAAR test. It consists of two basic types of instruction:

- **Guided instruction** materials offer annotations, citations from the Texas Essential Knowledge and Skills (TEKS), and answer explanations, plus models and rubrics for written composition. Annotations highlight the key skills you will need to apply. Sample questions, answer explanations, models, and rubrics help you analyze each question or prompt and its correct response.

- **Practice** materials give you the opportunity to apply what you have learned to assessments like those you will be taking near the end of your school year.

Part I is divided into the following sections:

Reading

The readings from a variety of genres give you opportunities to practice the essential reading skills outlined in the TEKS for your grade. Initially, as you read the Guided Reading passages, annotations and shading offer detailed explanations that draw attention to specific TEKS-based skills. After you have finished reading, you may review and hone test-taking skills by analyzing sample multiple-choice items, their answers, and answer explanations. You may also analyze short-answer questions with high-scoring response rubrics and sample answers. Following guided instruction, you will independently practice essential reading and assessment skills. For these Reading Practice lessons, you will read selections and answer multiple-choice items and short-answer questions that cover a range of appropriate TEKS and reading comprehension skills.

One feature of the Reading Practice materials in this book is a column headed "**My notes about what I am reading.**" You can improve your comprehension skills by using this column to monitor your reading abilities.

As you read the Reading Practice selections, take advantage of the "My notes about what I am reading" column by using it to make notes about the following topics.

- Key ideas or events

- Initial or overall impressions of characters, situations, or topics, including how each is like someone or something familiar to you

- Guesses at the meaning of any unfamiliar words or phrases

- Questions or points of confusion

- Ideas about why the author wrote the selection

- Comments about what you would like to know more about

- Your own ideas about the meaning of ideas or events or how they might apply to the real world

In addition, you may want to mark the selection text itself. You can, for example, circle, underscore, or highlight words or phrases that seem important or about which you have questions.

Written Composition

This section provides you with model essay prompts, sample essays, and scoring rubrics. These resources give you opportunities to practice the writing process for genres that will be tested. First, annotations will guide you as you analyze sample prompts and 2- and 4-point model responses. Then, you will practice your writing skills independently by responding to similar TEKS-aligned prompts.

Revising and Editing

In the multiple-choice format of this section, you will practice TEKS-based revising and editing skills. First, you will receive guided instruction in revising or editing. You will read sample essays, review assessment items, and analyze answer explanations. Then, you will work on independent practice, in which you identify editing or revising issues in sample essays and answer multiple-choice items crafted to cover a range of appropriate revising or editing TEKS.

PART II: *TEXAS WRITE SOURCE* ASSESSMENTS

The *Texas Write Source* assessments are a set of four tests designed to help you measure your progress in *Texas Write Source.*

- The **Pretest** should be completed at the beginning of the school year. It can help you measure your level of writing experience and knowledge and what your teacher might need to emphasize in your instruction. The **Pretest** also provides a baseline for measuring your progress from the beginning of the year to the end.

- **Progress Test 1** and **Progress Test 2** should be completed at regular intervals during the year. These tests can help you and your teacher monitor your progress as the school year proceeds.

- The **Post-test** should be completed at the end of the year to show how much progress you have made.

Each test has three parts. *Part 1: Improving Sentences and Paragraphs* and *Part 2: Correcting Sentence Errors* comprise a total of 32 multiple-choice questions. You will choose the best answer to each question. *Part 3: Writing* provides a writing prompt. You respond by writing a composition.

> NOTE: Every effort has been made to incorporate the latest information available about STAAR at the time of publication.

Part I

Preparing for Texas Assessments

Guided Reading

Reading Literary Text: Fiction

In this part of the book, you will read a short story with instruction about the elements of fiction. Following the selection are sample questions and answers about the story. The purpose of this section is to show you how to understand and analyze fiction.

To begin, review the TEKS that relate to fiction:

FICTION TEKS	WHAT IT MEANS TO YOU
(5) Comprehension of Literary Text/Fiction Students understand, make inferences and draw conclusions about the structure and elements of fiction and provide evidence from text to support their understanding. Students are expected to:	
(A) evaluate how different literary elements (e.g., figurative language, point of view) shape the author's portrayal of the plot and setting in works of fiction;	You will evaluate how authors use different literary elements, such as figurative language and point of view, to create the plot and setting in fictional works.
(B) analyze the internal and external development of characters through a range of literary devices;	You will analyze how characters are developed internally and externally through a variety of literary devices.
(C) analyze the impact of narration when the narrator's point of view shifts from one character to another; and	You will analyze how readers are affected when the narrator's point of view changes from one character to another.
(D) demonstrate familiarity with works by authors in American fiction from each major literary period.	You will become familiar with works by American writers from each major literary period.

The selection that follows provides instruction on the fiction TEKS as well as other TEKS. It also covers reading comprehension skills, such as making inferences and synthesizing ideas in text.

As you read the story "The Mentor," notice how the author develops the characters and the setting. The annotations in the margins will guide you as you read.

Name _____ Date _____

Guided Reading

Read this selection. Then answer the questions that follow.

The Mentor

1   "Why does everyone have to act like he's going to die!" said Matt, throwing his biscuit down so hard that it slopped gravy out of his plate and onto Granny's tablecloth—the hand-embroidered one that she put on for "comp'ny."

2   "Matthew!" cried his mother, emphasizing each syllable of his name. "Look what you've done!"

3   "Aw, don't worry 'bout that now," said Granny, distracted.

4   "Sorry," snapped Matt, his voice showing that he wasn't sorry at all. "But if you two keep up like that, talking about dying all the time, you're the ones who're going to kill him. God knows the things he's overheard." And with that Matt pushed away from the table and stomped from the kitchen.

5   He was still shaking when he reached Tobias Grider's hog lot, which adjoined his grandparents' property. He crossed through the barbed-wire fence carefully, remembering how Grandpa had taught him to pass a rifle through such a fence, to lean it butt down against one of the posts, to walk down the fence row "a piece," and then to separate the wires and climb through.

6   Matt and his grandfather had hunted together often. They had combed the woods for rabbits, squirrels, blackberries, and sassafras. They'd fished for bluegill, bass, perch, and crappie. They'd gone "dry land fishin'," as Grandpa put it, searching out those <u>prodigious</u> morel mushrooms that appear, as if spontaneously, in the dark, leafy humus after summer rains. Grandpa knew the ways of mushrooms. And of owls, fish, foxes, and even the moon. He knew about secret places in the earth, about caverns and springs. He knew a lot. More than I'll ever know, Matt thought.

7   For most of his seventeen years, Matt had been coming to see his grandfather from July through September. Summer after summer, the two had plumbed the hills and hollers together, the old man teaching without having to resort to words, the boy learning how to see and hear and smell and taste and feel as though he, himself, were a creature of the woods. Now, in mid-October, Matt had suddenly been called back from school. And for what reason? No reason. None.

SETTING AND POINT OF VIEW

The third-person limited narrator of this story shares Matt's thoughts and feelings with readers. In paragraph 6, Matt's impressions of the setting are intertwined with memories of his grandfather. Describing the landscape from Matt's point of view allows the author to bring the setting to life.

TEKS 5A

CONTEXT CLUES

Words with particular nuances, or subtle connotations, convey precise meanings. In paragraph 7, the word *plumbed* describes Matt and his grandfather's activities in the countryside. The author could have chosen the phrase *looked around*. However, the context indicates that Matt explored the area like "a creature of the woods." You can infer that *plumbed* means "examined carefully and deeply."

TEKS 1B

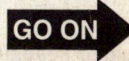
GO ON

8   Matt chased Tobias Grider's hogs, knowing that old Toby would bellow like a calving cow if he saw him. Matt didn't care. He chased the hogs some more. Tiring of that, he climbed through the fence on the opposite side of the lot. He made his way over a hill to a small pond that Toby and Matt's grandfather kept stocked with bait fish—minnows and chubs.

9   A late-summer growth of algae and lily pads choked the leeward side of the pond. Grasshoppers and crickets roared in the weeds. A bullfrog croaked, "Knee deep. Knee deep. Come in." That was Grandpa's joke. Grandpa loved the pond, saying the Garden of Eden had nothing on it. He could often be found sitting stock-still on the stump on the bank leaning over the water, just reflecting, he said. Matt smiled at the play on words, until thoughts of Grandpa's illness came rushing back. But, Grandpa had been sick before. Tuberculosis. It came and it went. All they had to do was quit anticipating his dying and look forward to his recovering. Idly, Matt gathered some stones for skimming, then abruptly dumped them into the pond. He wished he could get rid of this sudden heaviness in his heart so easily.

10   Coming back over the hill, he paused and looked long at his grandparents' house. Mother, Granny, and Great-Aunt Lucy were bunched up together on the front porch, like the three Fates, Mother on a cane-bottomed chair, Granny and Aunt Lucy on the porch swing with a bowl of snap beans between them. They were stringing and breaking up the beans for supper. His mother called to him, "Grandpa wants to see you."

11   Grandpa was sitting in bed, propped up with pillows. "Come over here, boy," he said, taking a deep breath as if to muster his strength. "I want to talk to you." Matt sat down on the stool beside the bed.

12   "You remember when you asked me straight out if I was dying?"

13   The boy nodded.

14   "I lied to you then. It was one of those lies people tell when they don't expect to be believed and it's easier to pretend. You know what I mean, don't you?"

15   The boy knew.

CHARACTER DEVELOPMENT

Authors may develop story characters externally, through their words and actions, or internally, by describing the characters' thoughts and feelings. At the beginning of the story, Matt speaks angrily to his family and storms out of the house. In paragraph 9, he relives fond memories of his grandfather. Consider what these details tell you about Matt.

TEKS 5B

ALLUSION

An allusion is a brief reference to something well-known, such as a famous person, event, or literary work. Paragraph 10 makes an allusion to the three Fates from classical mythology—powerful goddesses who determined the length of each person's life. The allusion emphasizes the growing likelihood of the grandfather's impending death.

TEKS 7

16   "I don't want there to be any lying between us. Not now. So I told your mother I'd talk to you." Grandpa grasped Matt's hand. Then he looked off into the distance. "I want you to think about an old tree that's been struck down by lightning or disease or just plain tiredness. It lies there for a long time, and it rots. And a million tiny bundles of life—insects, funguses, molds, plants of all kinds—feed on it. Maybe some fox or bird builds a nest in the trunk. Life goes on, and death makes it possible, makes it what it is."

17   Matt wanted to say something but couldn't. The weight in his heart had become a lump in his throat. Grandpa looked back at him and smiled gently.

18   "The way I figure it, when an old person dies, a young person learns that death is real. And that knowledge makes the child into a man or a woman who understands how precious life is, who lives fully and completely without compromises.

19   "You're going to be like that, boy. That's what I leave to you. That's what you do for me. Now go out and let me rest."

20   Matt's mother went into town to buy groceries, though there really wasn't anything the family needed. Not long after, Aunt Lucy went to check on Grandpa and came rushing out to get Granny. It seemed like hours later when Granny and Aunt Lucy emerged from the bedroom—two suddenly shrunken old ladies, propping each other up. Matt's eyes swam with tears. He rose from the sofa and went out to the front porch, the screen door slamming behind him. He bit down hard, fixing his childhood memories forever in his mind to keep him company as a man. Around him, the sun shone, geese honked on their way south, and the leaves whispered and fell.

THEME
The specific details of a story point to a message, or theme, that is usually a view or comment on the human condition. Consider how the view of life that Grandpa expresses in paragraph 18 might relate to a theme of the story.

TEKS 2A

Use "The Mentor" (pp. 5–7) to answer questions 1–6.

---

1 What impression of this story's setting does the third-person limited point of view help convey?

A It is a rural area full of natural wonders and secrets to be learned.

B It is an economically poor region that most young people would not find stimulating.

C It is a small town that Matt finds depressing because of its association with death and dying.

D It is a landscape that Matt enjoyed as a child but no longer cherishes.

EXPLANATION: The narrator reveals Matt's thoughts and memories as he roams the rural area he has explored during summers with his grandfather. In paragraph 6, Matt recalls with admiration that "Grandpa knew the ways of mushrooms. And of owls, fish, foxes, and even the moon. He knew about secret places in the earth, about caverns and springs." **A** is correct.

- **B** is incorrect. Although the region may be economically poor, it is portrayed through Matt's eyes as very stimulating because of its natural features and the knowledge Grandpa has shared about it.
- **C** is incorrect. The hog lot, hunting, and fishing suggest a rural area rather than a small town. Also, while Matt feels sad about his grandfather's illness, the story does not suggest that he finds the setting depressing. Instead, the natural surroundings hold all of Matt's fondest memories with Grandpa.
- **D** is incorrect. Matt still takes comfort in spending time at the pond and even chasing hogs at the hog lot. From the way he recalls hunting and fishing with his grandfather in paragraph 6, readers can infer that he is still interested in these activities.

TEKS 5A; Fig. 19B

2 One meaning of the word <u>prodigious</u> is "very large." Based on the context of paragraph 6, you can infer that another nuance of the word's meaning is —

F inedible

G aquatic

H marvelous

J obvious

EXPLANATION: The morel mushrooms spring up "as if spontaneously . . . after summer rains." This is a surprising and marvelous natural event that Matt learns about from his grandfather. **H** is correct.

- **F** is incorrect because there would be no reason to hunt for the mushrooms if they were not edible.
- **G** is incorrect. The mushrooms grow after rainfall, but there are no clues to indicate that they grow in a pond or other body of water.
- **J** is incorrect. If the mushrooms were obvious, Grandpa and Matt would not have to search for them.

TEKS 1B

3 What does the allusion to the Garden of Eden in paragraph 9 show about Grandpa's view of the pond?

A He loves the pond because it brings back childhood memories and ideals.

B He believes that a pond like this was where all life began.

C He sees the pond as a wonderful place and a source of life.

D He believes there are snakes in the pond.

EXPLANATION: In the Bible, the Garden of Eden is an earthly paradise, full of plants and animals living in harmony. The pond, which Grandpa loves, is also full of living things. By comparing the pond to the Garden of Eden, Grandpa suggests that it is like paradise to him as well as a source of life for many plants and animals. **C** is correct.

• **A** is incorrect because Grandpa's childhood memories are not included in the story.

• **B** is incorrect. No evidence suggests that Grandpa thinks life began in a pond.

• **D** is incorrect. Grandpa loves the pond; when he makes his comparison, he is not thinking of the evil serpent in the Garden of Eden.

TEKS 7; Fig. 19B

4 Read the following passage from the story.

> ". . . And that knowledge makes the child into a man or a woman who understands how precious life is, who lives fully and completely without compromises.
>
> "You're going to be like that, boy. That's what I leave to you. That's what you do for me. Now go out and let me rest."

What do Grandpa's words reveal about him?

F He is very tired and wants Matt to leave the room so he can sleep.

G He believes Matt will soon forget about him and will lead a happier life than his own.

H He knows his death will hurt Matt but also thinks it will give him a better perspective on life.

J He has left Matt a large inheritance in his will, which the boy will learn about after he has died.

EXPLANATION: Grandpa is being honest with Matt about the fact that he is dying, but he wants Matt to know that there is something positive to be gained from this experience. Knowing that death is inevitable makes life all the more precious. **H** is correct.

• **F** is incorrect. Although he asks Matt to leave so he can rest, this is not the main idea of his comments.

• **G** is incorrect. Nothing in the story suggests that Grandpa expects Matt to forget him or that Grandpa has not had a happy life.

• **J** is incorrect. What Grandpa leaves to Matt is the wisdom to accept death, not a literal inheritance.

TEKS 5B; Fig. 19B

GO ON ➡

5 Which statement expresses a main theme of the story?

A Death comes unexpectedly.

B Family members should not lie to one another.

C Human beings who fight their fate are worthy of admiration.

D We must accept death as part of the natural cycle of life.

EXPLANATION: The story focuses on Matt's initial refusal to accept that his grandfather is dying and his eventual acceptance of the situation. Grandpa has always taught Matt about nature, and his analogy to the dead tree in paragraph 16 supports the view of nature as a cycle in which death supports new life. **D** is correct.

- **A** is incorrect. Grandpa's death is not unexpected; Matt is just having trouble accepting it.
- **B** is incorrect. Grandpa first told Matt that he was not dying before later telling him the truth, but lying is not the focus of the story.
- **C** is incorrect. Grandpa does not fight his fate but accepts it as part of the natural cycle of life. Matt's initial refusal to accept his grandfather's fate is not depicted as something worthy of admiration.

TEKS 2A; Fig. 19A, 19B

6 Which of the following excerpts from the story is an example of internal character development that shows how close Matt is to his grandfather?

F *And with that Matt pushed away from the table and stomped from the kitchen.*

G *Matt didn't care. He chased the hogs some more.*

H *Idly, Matt gathered some stones for skimming, then abruptly dumped them into the pond.*

J *He wished he could get rid of this sudden heaviness in his heart so easily.*

EXPLANATION: Internal character development means showing readers what a character is like by revealing the character's thoughts and feelings. **J** is correct because it tells what Matt is wishing and it tells readers that his heart is heavy because his beloved grandfather is dying.

- **F** and **H** are incorrect because both describe Matt's actions, making them examples of external character development.
- **G** is incorrect. Although it describes Matt's internal attitude about something, it does not relate directly to his close relationship with his grandfather.

TEKS 5B

Answer the following question in the space provided.

---

7 Trace the internal and external development of Matt's character throughout the story. How does his attitude change as he struggles to cope with the death of his grandfather and mentor?

EXPLANATION

Rubric, high-scoring response:
- Reflects a perceptive awareness of the text's meaning and complexities; makes meaningful connections across the text
- Uses specific, well-chosen evidence from the text, supporting validity of response
- Shows deep understanding of the text through ideas and supporting text evidence

Sample Response: In the beginning of the story, Matt is angry with the rest of his family for behaving as if Grandpa is dying: He throws down his biscuit and exclaims, "Why does everyone have to act like he's going to die!" After he stomps from the kitchen and crosses the land his grandfather taught him to love, he continues to deny the situation to himself: "Now, in mid-October, Matt had suddenly been called back from school. And for what reason? No reason. None." But he cannot escape the truth. At the pond, a "sudden heaviness in his heart" reflects his growing recognition that his grandfather is gravely ill. In the end, it is his talk with Grandpa that helps Matt fully accept the situation. When his grandfather dies, Matt's eyes fill with tears, but he also goes out to experience the ongoing cycle of nature that his grandfather taught him so much about—the shining sun, the geese honking on their way south, the falling leaves. Matt will always cherish his childhood memories of his grandfather, but now he has become a man.

TEKS 2A, 5B; Fig. 19A, 19B

Reading Literary Text: Literary Nonfiction

In this part of the book, you will read a speech with instruction about the elements of literary nonfiction. Following the selection are sample questions and answers about the speech.
The purpose of this section is to show you how to understand and analyze literary nonfiction.

To begin, review the TEKS that relate to literary nonfiction:

LITERARY NONFICTION TEKS	WHAT IT MEANS TO YOU
(6) Comprehension of Literary Text/Literary Nonfiction Students understand, make inferences and draw conclusions about the varied structural patterns and features of literary nonfiction and provide evidence from text to support their understanding. Students are expected to analyze how rhetorical techniques (e.g., repetition, parallel structure, understatement, overstatement) in literary essays, true life adventures, and historically important speeches influence the reader, evoke emotions, and create meaning.	You will understand, make inferences, and draw conclusions about the structure and features of literary nonfiction and support your analysis with evidence from the text. You will analyze the ways that rhetorical devices, such as repetition, parallel structure, understatement, and overstatement, in literary essays, real life adventures, and historically important speeches affect readers and convey a message.

The selection that follows provides instruction on the literary nonfiction TEKS as well as other TEKS. It also covers reading comprehension skills, such as summarizing and synthesizing information and making complex inferences based on textual evidence.

As you read President Franklin D. Roosevelt's "Address on the Declaration of War on Japan," notice how Roosevelt's use of language conveys his message in a powerful way. The annotations in the margins will guide you as you read.

Name _____ Date _____

Guided Reading

Read this selection. Then answer the questions that follow.

---

from Presidential Address on the Declaration of War on Japan

by Franklin D. Roosevelt

After Japanese planes attacked Pearl Harbor in Hawaii, the United States declared war on Japan on December 8, 1941. The next day, President Roosevelt explained the decision to the American people in the following radio address.

1   The sudden criminal attacks perpetrated by the Japanese in the Pacific provide the climax of a decade of international immorality.

2   Powerful and resourceful gangsters have banded together to make war upon the whole human race. Their challenge has now been flung at the United States of America. The Japanese have treacherously violated the long-standing peace between us. Many American soldiers and sailors have been killed by enemy action. American ships have been sunk; American airplanes have been destroyed.

3   The Congress and the people of the United States have accepted that challenge.

4   Together with other free peoples, we are now fighting to maintain our right to live among our world neighbors in freedom, in common decency, without fear of assault.

5   I have prepared the full record of our past relations with Japan, and it will be submitted to the Congress. It begins with the visit of Commodore Perry to Japan 88 years ago. It ends with the visit of two Japanese <u>emissaries</u> to the Secretary of State last Sunday, an hour after Japanese forces had loosed their bombs and machine guns against our flag, our forces, and our citizens.

6   I can say with utmost confidence that no Americans today or a thousand years hence, need feel anything but pride in our patience and our efforts through all the years toward achieving a peace in the Pacific which would be fair and honorable to every nation, large or small. And no honest person, today or a thousand years hence, will be able to

DICTION AND TONE
Notice President Roosevelt's diction, or choice of words, in paragraphs 1 and 2. He uses words such as *criminal, immorality, gangsters, treacherously,* and *enemy* to describe the Japanese attack on Pearl Harbor. These words clearly convey his tone, or attitude, toward the Japanese government and its actions. Think about how his diction and tone relate to his purpose in the speech.

TEKS 8

suppress a sense of indignation and horror at the treachery committed by the military dictators of Japan, under the very shadow of the flag of peace borne by their special envoys in our midst.

7   The course that Japan has followed for the past 10 years in Asia has paralleled the course of Hitler and Mussolini in Europe and in Africa. Today, it has become far more than a parallel. It is actual collaboration so well calculated that all the continents of the world, and all the oceans, are now considered by the Axis strategists as one gigantic battlefield.

8   In 1931, ten years ago, Japan invaded Manchukuo—without warning.

9   In 1935, Italy invaded Ethiopia—without warning.

10   In 1938, Hitler occupied Austria—without warning.

11   In 1939, Hitler invaded Czechoslovakia—without warning.

12   Later in '39, Hitler invaded Poland—without warning.

13   In 1940, Hitler invaded Norway, Denmark, the Netherlands, Belgium, and Luxembourg—without warning.

14   In 1940, Italy attacked France and later Greece—without warning.

15   And this year, in 1941, the Axis Powers attacked Yugoslavia and Greece and they dominated the Balkans—without warning.

16   In 1941, also, Hitler invaded Russia—without warning.

17   And now Japan has attacked Malaya and Thailand—and the United States—without warning.

18   It is all of one pattern.

19   We are now in this war. We are all in it—all the way. Every single man, woman, and child is a partner in the most tremendous undertaking of our American history. We must share together the bad news and the good news, the defeats and the victories—the changing fortunes of war.

20   . . . We expect to eliminate the danger from Japan, but it would serve us ill if we accomplished that and found that the rest of the world was dominated by Hitler and Mussolini.

21   So we are going to win the war and we are going to win the peace that follows. . . .

CONTEXT CLUES

The word *collaboration* (paragraph 7) may not be familiar. However, since the context suggests that Japan, Hitler, and Mussolini were working together, you can infer that *collaboration* means "the act of working together." Knowing that the Latin prefix *co-* means "with" or "together" provides another clue to the word's meaning.

TEKS 1A, 1B

RHETORICAL DEVICES

The use of repetition and parallel structure can help drive home the points a speaker or writer wishes to make. For example, in paragraphs 8–17, Roosevelt uses parallel structure and repetition of the phrase "without warning." Consider the point he is trying to make and the impact this rhetorical device would have on listeners.

TEKS 6

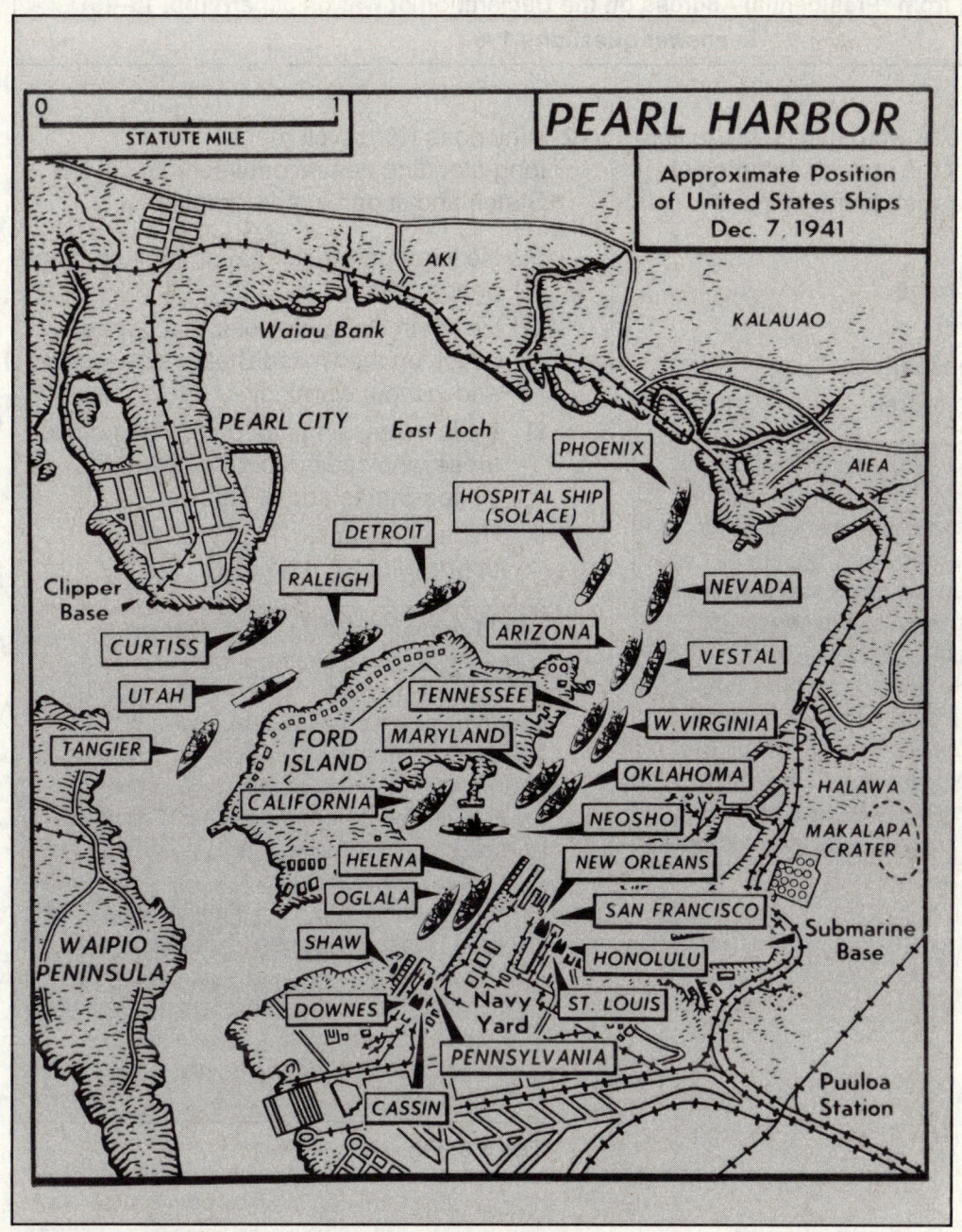

PEARL HARBOR

Approximate Position of United States Ships Dec. 7, 1941

This map shows the positions of U.S. battleships in Pearl Harbor at the time of the Japanese attack.

Use the excerpt from "Presidential Address on the Declaration of War on Japan" (pp. 13–15) to answer questions 1–8.

1 Examine Roosevelt's word choice in the first two paragraphs of the speech. What chief emotions does he wish to evoke in his audience?

A Anger and outrage

B Fear and worry

C Sorrow and despair

D Nostalgia and regret

> **EXPLANATION:** In using words like *criminal, immorality, gangsters,* and *treacherously* to describe Japan's actions, Roosevelt wants to make sure the American public shares his sense of outrage at the attack that resulted in the loss of American lives. **A** is correct.
> • **B** and **C** are incorrect. Roosevelt has declared war. He wants to inspire confidence in victory, not make the public worry or feel despair.
> • **D** is incorrect. Nothing in the passage expresses a longing for the past or questions past actions by the United States.

TEKS 6, 8; Fig. 19B

2 Why does Roosevelt mention "the long-standing peace" between the United States and Japan in paragraph 2?

F He is preparing the nation for last-minute peace talks.

G He is stressing his point that Japan's attack on the United States was sudden and without warning.

H He is expressing a counterargument to those who seek peace between the United States and Japan.

J He is being ironic and means the opposite of what he says.

> **EXPLANATION:** Reminding listeners of the long-standing peaceful relationship, including Commodore Perry's peaceful visit to Japan and the ongoing peace talks with the Japanese (paragraph 5), stresses the sudden, surprising nature of the attack. **G** is correct.
> • **F** is incorrect. Roosevelt is explaining the reasons for declaring war, not preparing the nation for peace talks.
> • **H** is incorrect. At no point in the speech does Roosevelt address those who seek peace with Japan.
> • **J** is incorrect. Roosevelt is simply reminding listeners of past events. To use irony or sarcasm would undermine his serious tone in this speech.

TEKS 8; Fig. 19B

GO ON

3 What is Roosevelt's main purpose in making this speech to the American public?

A To mourn the loss of American troops

B To pay tribute to the valiant efforts of Ethiopia, Poland, and other nations that the Axis powers have invaded

C To remind listeners of the past relationship between the United States and Japan

D To persuade his audience to support the war

EXPLANATION: In this speech, Roosevelt carefully lays out his and Congress's reasons for declaring war on Japan so that the public will understand and support the decision. **D** is correct.

- **A** is incorrect. Roosevelt mentions the loss of American soldiers and sailors as part of the justification for going to war, but his main purpose in this speech is to rally the nation, not lead it in mourning.

- **B** is incorrect. Roosevelt mentions the invasion of those nations and others as examples of Axis aggression, not to praise the efforts of those nations to resist invasion.

- **C** is incorrect. Roosevelt sums up the past relationship between the United States and Japan, but his concern is Japan's recent attack and its potential future behavior as an Axis power.

TEKS 8; Fig. 19A, 19B

4 Emissaries (paragraph 5) is from the Latin root *mit,* which means "send." Based on your understanding of the root and the context in which the word appears, what does *emissaries* mean?

F Tourists visiting a foreign nation for the first time

G Politicians making speeches

H Diplomats sent abroad with messages to foreign governments

J Government documents sent to an ally nation

EXPLANATION: From the context of the paragraph, you can tell that emissaries have come from Japan to negotiate with the Secretary of State. Their actions, as well as the root *mit,* suggest that they were sent by the Japanese government. **H** is correct.

- **F** is incorrect because tourists would not ordinarily meet with the Secretary of State.

- **G** is incorrect. The emissaries have been meeting with the Secretary of State, not making speeches.

- **J** is incorrect. The context makes it clear that the word refers to people, not documents.

TEKS 1A, 1B

GO ON

5 Which of the following best summarizes the point Roosevelt is making with his use of repetition and parallelism in paragraphs 8–17?

A Hitler and Mussolini have engaged in a pattern of attacks without warning for the past ten years. Now Japan has joined the Axis powers, and the United States must take action to stop them.

B Attacks without warning by Axis powers have been taking place for ten years, but now they are becoming more frequent. Therefore, the United States must join the war.

C The attack on Pearl Harbor is only the latest in a ten-year history of attacks by Axis powers, which are acting in collaboration. The pattern will continue if the United States does not take action.

D The attacks by Axis powers are random and unpredictable. It is impossible for the United States to know who its allies and enemies are. Therefore, the nation must go to war against the whole world.

EXPLANATION: In paragraph 7, Roosevelt says that the Japanese have been acting in collaboration with Hitler and Mussolini for the past ten years. In paragraph 18, he summarizes his series of parallel statements by stating, "It is all of one pattern." **C** is correct.
- **A** is incorrect. The first invasion without warning that Roosevelt mentions is by Japan in 1931, so the Japanese are not just joining the Axis now.
- **B** is incorrect because Roosevelt emphasizes not the frequency but the consistency of the pattern.
- **D** is incorrect because Roosevelt is clear about who the enemies of the United States are: Japan, Germany, and Italy, or the Axis powers.

TEKS 6; Fig. 19A

6 What inference or conclusion does Roosevelt expect his audience to draw from his statement in paragraph 20?

F The United States must go to war with Germany and Italy as well as Japan.

G The United States must go to war with Japan but not with Germany and Italy.

H The United States will not be able to defeat Japan if Germany and Italy become Japan's allies in the future.

J With so many enemies allied against the United States, diplomacy would be wiser than warfare.

EXPLANATION: Roosevelt has spoken of the collaboration of Japan, Germany, and Italy and has cited many examples to prove the pattern of unprovoked invasions and attacks. He points out that it would be "ill," or bad, to defeat Japan and still face a world dominated by Germany and Italy. He wants the audience to conclude that the United States must fight all three Axis nations. **F** is correct.
- **G** is incorrect. It says the opposite of what Roosevelt means.
- **H** is incorrect. Roosevelt expresses confidence in victory, and he explains that Japan is already working in collaboration with Germany and Italy.
- **J** is incorrect. Roosevelt is declaring war, not recommending diplomacy.

TEKS 6; Fig. 19B

GO ON

7 Which of the following is an accurate statement based on the map on page 15?

  A Most American battleships in Pearl Harbor had names borrowed from the Hawaiian language.

  B About half of the U.S. naval fleet was stationed in Pearl Harbor at the time of the Japanese attack.

  C Pearl Harbor was a base for both battleships and submarines in 1941.

  D The U.S. military built railroad tracks around Pearl Harbor to transport supplies to the naval fleet.

> **EXPLANATION:** The map's caption identifies the ships in the harbor as U.S. battleships, and a submarine base is identified near Puuloa Station. **C** is correct.
> - **A** is incorrect. The only ship that has a Hawaiian name is the *Honolulu.* Most others are named after places in the continental United States (*California, New Orleans*) or naval officers (*Shaw, Downes*).
> - **B** is incorrect. It is not possible to tell from the map what fraction of the U.S. fleet is represented by the battleships in Pearl Harbor.
> - **D** is incorrect. Although the harbor is surrounded by railroad tracks, the map does not indicate who built them.

TEKS 11B

8 What does the map add to your understanding of Roosevelt's message in his speech?

  F It emphasizes the scale of the Japanese attack by indicating how many "American soldiers and sailors [were] killed by enemy action."

  G It underscores his message that the Japanese attack was treacherous and unexpected, since the U.S. Navy left itself vulnerable by gathering so many battleships in one place.

  H It illustrates the steady march of Japanese aggression from Manchukuo to Malaya and Thailand to the southern Pacific, suggesting that the U.S. mainland will be the next target.

  J It lends credibility to his statement that "we are going to win the war" by showing that the U.S. Navy has a large number of battleships.

> **EXPLANATION:** The map shows a large number of battleships gathered in one place. If the United States had expected an attack on Pearl Harbor, it would have moved the ships from the harbor so that the fleet could not be devastated in a single attack. **G** is correct.
> - **F** is incorrect. The map provides no information about the number of soldiers and sailors killed in the attack.
> - **H** is incorrect. The map shows only Pearl Harbor, so it cannot show the progress of the Japanese military campaign from Asia to the southern Pacific or suggest where it might spread next.
> - **J** is incorrect. The map shows how many battleships were in Pearl Harbor just before the attack, but many of these ships were destroyed.

TEKS 12; Fig. 19A

GO ON ➡

Name _____ Date _____

9 Citing examples, explain how Roosevelt uses repetition and parallel structure to emphasize his main points.

EXPLANATION

Rubric, high-scoring response:
- Reflects a perceptive awareness of the text's meaning and complexities; makes meaningful connections across the text
- Uses specific, well-chosen evidence from the text, supporting validity of response
- Shows deep understanding of the text through ideas and supporting text evidence

Sample Response: Roosevelt uses repetition and parallel structure to make the case for war to the American public. In his opening paragraphs, repetition and parallel structure help emphasize the destructiveness of the Japanese attack: "American ships have been sunk; American airplanes have been destroyed." In paragraph 6, Roosevelt uses repetition and parallel structure to contrast American efforts at peace with the Japanese treachery of attacking the United States during those peace talks: "[N]o Americans today or a thousand years hence, need feel anything but pride in our patience and our efforts through all the years toward achieving a peace in the Pacific. . . . And no honest person, today or a thousand years hence, will be able to suppress a sense of indignation and horror at the treachery committed by the military dictators of Japan, under the very shadow of the flag of peace. . . ." In paragraphs 8–17, Roosevelt uses repetition and parallel structure to drive home his message about a "pattern" of Axis surprise attacks. And he uses repetition and parallel structure to make his concluding message of hope for the future more memorable: "So we are going to win the war and we are going to win the peace that follows."

TEKS 6; Fig. 19A, 19B

Reading Literary Text: Poetry

In this part of the book, you will read a poem with instruction about the elements of poetry. Following the selection are sample questions and answers about the poem. The purpose of this section is to show you how to understand and analyze poetry.

To begin, review the TEKS that relate to poetry:

POETRY TEKS	WHAT IT MEANS TO YOU
(3) Comprehension of Literary Text/Poetry Students understand, make inferences and draw conclusions about the structure and elements of poetry and provide evidence from text to support their understanding. Students are expected to analyze the effects of metrics, rhyme schemes (e.g., end, internal, slant, eye), and other conventions in American poetry.	You will understand, make inferences, and draw conclusions about the structure and elements of poetry and support your analysis with evidence from the text. You will analyze the effects of meter, rhyme, and other poetic techniques in American poetry.

The selection that follows provides instruction on the poetry TEKS as well as other TEKS. It also covers reading comprehension skills, such as making complex inferences based on evidence in the text.

As you read the poem "A Bird Came Down the Walk," notice how the poet uses the elements of poetry. The annotations in the margin will guide you as you read.

Name _____ Date _____

Guided Reading

> Read this selection. Then answer the questions that follow.

A Bird Came Down the Walk

by Emily Dickinson

A Bird came down the Walk—
He did not know I saw—
He bit an Angleworm in halves
And ate the fellow, raw,

5 And then he drank a Dew
From a convenient Grass—
And then hopped sidewise to the Wall
To let a Beetle pass—

He glanced with rapid eyes
10 That hurried all around—
They looked like frightened Beads, I thought—
He stirred his Velvet Head

Like one in danger, Cautious,
I offered him a Crumb,
15 And he unrolled his feathers
And rowed him softer home—

Than Oars divide the Ocean,
Too silver for a seam—
Or Butterflies, off Banks of Noon
20 Leap, plashless as they swim.

ELEMENTS OF POETRY
Notice the metric pattern and rhyme scheme of the poem's first stanza: The first, second, and fourth lines are iambic trimeter (three beats to a line); the third line is iambic tetrameter (four beats to a line); and the second and fourth lines rhyme (*saw/raw*). In some stanzas, the end rhymes are slant or near rhymes: *around/head* (lines 10 and 12).

TEKS 3

SENSORY LANGUAGE
Lines 15–20 use vivid imagery and figurative language to describe how the bird flies off when the speaker offers it food. Consider how effectively the imagery helps capture the flight of the bird.

TEKS 7

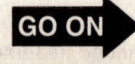

Use "A Bird Came Down the Walk" (p. 22) to answer questions 1–6.

1 Which of these word pairs forms a slant rhyme in the rhyme scheme of the poem?

- **A** *saw/raw* (lines 2 and 4)
- **B** *Grass/pass* (lines 6 and 8)
- **C** *Crumb/home* (lines 14 and 16)
- **D** *Ocean/swim* (lines 17 and 20)

EXPLANATION: In the rhyme scheme of the poem, the second and fourth lines of each stanza have end rhymes. *Crumb* and *home* end the second and fourth lines of the fourth stanza, and they rhyme imperfectly. **C** is correct.
- **A** and **B** are incorrect. The word pairs are part of the poem's rhyme scheme, but the words in each pair form perfect rhymes, not slant rhymes.
- **D** is incorrect. *Ocean* and *swim* might be considered to form a slant rhyme, but they do not end the second and fourth lines of their stanza and so do not fall into the poem's rhyme scheme.

TEKS 3

2 Which aspect of the poem's content do its short trimeter and tetrameter lines most clearly reflect or capture?

- **F** The bird's movements and behavior
- **G** The bird's velvety feathers
- **H** The bird's soaring through the sky
- **J** The poem's setting

EXPLANATION: The bird's abrupt movements and startling behavior are echoed by the short lines of the poem. **F** is correct.
- **G** and **H** are incorrect. The bird's velvety feathers and soaring flight are soft, graceful images that would be reflected by long, smooth lines and not abrupt, short ones.
- **J** is incorrect. There is little relationship between the short lines and the setting.

TEKS 3; Fig. 19A

3 Read the following dictionary entry.

bank \băngk\ *n.* **1.** a heap of snow **2.** a stretch of rising land at the edge of a body of water **3.** the cushion around a billiards table **4.** the tilting of a vehicle as it makes a sharp turn

What is the definition of <u>banks</u> as it is used in line 19 of the poem?

- **A** Definition 1
- **B** Definition 2
- **C** Definition 3
- **D** Definition 4

EXPLANATION: B is correct. The last two lines compare the bird's flight to butterflies "swimming" in the sun. In this context, the "Banks of Noon" would be the sunny edges of the imaginary bodies of water in which the butterflies swim. **A**, **C**, and **D** are incorrect because they do not relate to this image of butterflies swimming.

TEKS 1E

4 How does the imagery in the last six lines differ from the imagery in lines 1–14?

F It is less awe-inspiring.

G It is more beautiful.

H It is more earthly and dull.

J It is more rural.

EXPLANATION: The first six lines contain mostly unpleasant images—the bird biting a worm in half and eating it raw, letting a beetle pass, and glancing with rapid eyes "like frightened Beads." The last six lines use vivid images to capture the beauty and wonder of the bird's flight. **G** is correct.

- **F** is incorrect. The bird's soaring through the sky and the butterflies to which it is compared are quite awe-inspiring.
- **H** is incorrect. The soaring bird and "swimming" butterflies are not at all dull. The earlier images are more earthly.
- **J** is incorrect. The last six lines describe actions in the sky; there is nothing particularly rural about them.

TEKS 3, 7

5 Enjambment is a poetic technique in which a sentence or clause continues from one line or stanza to the next. Which of the following ideas is clarified when the reader notices Dickinson's use of enjambment?

A The speaker sees the bird, but the bird does not see the speaker at first.

B The bird drinks some dew after eating the angle-worm.

C The bird acts like one in danger, not the speaker.

D The bird glances with quick eyes that look everywhere in a rush.

EXPLANATION: Lines 12 and 13, "He stirred his Velvet Head / Like one in danger . . .," form a complete clause that breaks across the third and fourth stanzas. A reader who fails to notice the enjambment might think that "Like one in danger" refers to the speaker, who offers the bird a crumb in line 14. **C** is correct.

- **A** and **D** are incorrect because in both cases each idea is expressed in a separate clause in its own line.
- **B** is incorrect. The bird eats the worm in the first stanza, which ends with a period. The second stanza presents the bird's next action of drinking the dew.

TEKS 3

GO ON ➡

6 Through the events and imagery in this poem, what general comment best expresses Dickinson's message about nature?

F Nature is easily tamed.

G Nature is comforting.

H Nature is simple and clear.

J Nature is mysterious.

EXPLANATION: The speaker is first startled by the bird's behavior, then puzzled by its rejection of the crumb, and finally awed by the bird's graceful flight. Viewing the bird as representative of nature, **J** is correct.

- **F** is incorrect. The bird's rejection of the crumb suggests that nature is not easily tamed.
- **G** is incorrect. The bird's startling behavior in eating the raw worm, rejecting the food, and abruptly flying off suggests that nature is disconcerting, not comforting.
- **H** is incorrect. The bird's behavior puzzles the speaker, and its final flight is described in terms of wonder and mystery. The details suggest that nature is not at all simple or clear.

TEKS 2A, 3; Fig. 19A

GO ON

Answer the following question in the space provided.

---

7 Emily Dickinson lived a simple life, rarely venturing from home, yet she was able to draw on her limited experience to make profound observations about the human condition. Explain how "A Bird Came Down the Walk" draws on an everyday experience to express profound ideas.

EXPLANATION
Rubric, high-scoring response:
- Reflects a perceptive awareness of the text's meaning and complexities; makes meaningful connections across the text
- Uses specific, well-chosen evidence from the text, supporting validity of response
- Shows deep understanding of the text through ideas and supporting text evidence

Sample Response: In "A Bird Came Down the Walk," Emily Dickinson draws on observations of everyday events to make profound observations about nature and human experience. She begins with a startling yet common image: A bird on the speaker's walk bites a worm in half and eats it raw. The bird continues with its everyday activities, drinking some dew and avoiding a beetle. The bird has eyes "like frightened Beads," and when the speaker offers it food, it abruptly flies away. Here Dickinson's imagination also takes flight, for she describes the bird's departure in highly imaginative terms, likening the pumping of its wings to rowing home more softly and seamlessly "Than Oars divide the Ocean" and further comparing the bird to butterflies leaping and swimming, without splashing, off "Banks of Noon." By the end of the poem, the bird has become all of untamed nature, full of mystery and wonder, and the speaker—and reader—have undergone a spiritual experience in admiring yet failing to understand it. By moving from the earthly to the sublime, the poem implies that almost any everyday experience has great wonders to teach human beings and that all of creation is an awe-inspiring mystery.

TEKS 2A, 3, 7; Fig. 19A

Reading Literary Text: Drama

In this part of the book, you will read a play with instruction about the elements of drama. Following the selection are sample questions and answers about the play. The purpose of this section is to show you how to understand and analyze drama.

To begin, review the TEKS that relate to drama:

DRAMA TEKS	WHAT IT MEANS TO YOU
(4) Comprehension of Literary Text/Drama Students understand, make inferences and draw conclusions about the structure and elements of drama and provide evidence from text to support their understanding. Students are expected to analyze the themes and characteristics in different periods of modern American drama.	You will understand, make inferences, and draw conclusions about the structure and elements of drama and support your analysis with evidence from the text. You will analyze the themes and distinctive elements of different periods in modern American drama.

The selection that follows provides instruction on the drama TEKS as well as other TEKS. It also covers reading comprehension skills, such as making complex inferences about text.

As you read the play *Something's Changed,* notice how the author uses dialogue and stage directions to tell a story with a theme about life. The annotations in the margins will guide you as you read.

Name _____ Date _____

Read this selection. Then answer the questions that follow.

Something's Changed

CAST

Sylvia Sole, a sixteen-year-old high school student

Mr. Sole, her dad

Mrs. Sole, her mom

Pearl, Sylvia's best friend

Mike, Sylvia's friend

Dan, a popular football player

Scene 1

Sylvia: *(flinging herself into the kitchen and holding her hand to her forehead)* I don't feel up to school today!

Mr. Sole: *(not looking up from his paper)* Okay, honey. Could you pass me the milk?

5 **Mrs. Sole:** *(to her husband)* Do you want cereal or toast for breakfast?

Sylvia: Does anyone ever listen to me? *(She flounces back to her bedroom, where she gazes at herself in the mirror.)* Truly, sometimes, I think I am invisible. I am just a vision
10 of . . . of . . . ordinariness! *(Holds up a hank of hair)* I mean, look at this hair—could it be a duller color? I've seen mud with better highlights. I know I am a tad prone to exaggeration, but I am getting tired of blending into the scenery. Just once I would like to be noticed, especially by Dan.

15 **Mrs. Sole:** Sylvia, hurry or you'll miss your bus!

Sylvia: *(throwing her backpack over her shoulder)* And don't get me started on my name! Could you have thought of anything more old-fashioned to call me?

STAGE DIRECTIONS
When you read a play, pay attention to the stage directions, which are italicized and in parentheses. Stage directions describe the characters' body language, manner of speech, and movements. Sylvia's entrance suggests that she is quite dramatic.

TEKS 4

ELEMENTS OF DRAMA
The major conflict, or struggle, in a play is often introduced in the beginning. In lines 7–14, Sylvia reveals her conflict over feeling "invisible" and ordinary.

TEKS 4

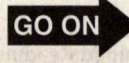
GO ON

Mrs. Sole: Hey, as you often quote to me, "A rose by any
20 other name would smell as sweet." Although, sweet is not the
word I would use to describe you right now!

Sylvia: Bye, Mom.

Scene 2

*A hallway in school. Sylvia walks with her friends Pearl and
Mike.*

25 **Pearl:** I can't believe you got the lead in the musical, Sylvia! I
always knew your drama-queen <u>tendency</u> would take you far!
Not to mention your musical talent, of course!

Sylvia: I am so excited. I was sure the lead would go to a
senior.

30 **Mike:** You have the best voice in school, Sylvia. No one else
could be Maria in *West Side Story* but you.

Sylvia: *(suddenly shy)* Do you really think so? Thank you,
Mike.

(Lights fade on the three friends.)

Scene 3

35 *Pearl and Sylvia in Sylvia's bedroom after school.*

Sylvia: Pearl, getting the lead has given me the confidence I
need to make a momentous change. I am going blonde.

Pearl: Don't tell me—it's to attract Dan, isn't it? But, you two
have nothing in common. He is really into sports and cars,
40 and you're not. Plus, do you really want to go out with
someone who only looks at you because of your hair color?

Sylvia: I feel sure that we are kindred spirits underneath.
I just have to get him to see me.

Pearl: I still think you should go out with Mike.

ALLUSION

An allusion is an indirect reference to a famous person, place, event, or literary work. In lines 19–20, Mrs. Sole quotes a line from Shakespeare's *Romeo and Juliet* to remind her daughter that her name should make no difference to who she is.

TEKS 7

ELEMENTS OF DRAMA

In a play, dialogue, or the conversation between characters, reveals each character's qualities. In lines 25–31, you learn that Sylvia is a talented singer.

TEKS 4

CONTEXT CLUES

If you are uncertain of the meaning of *kindred* in line 42, look at what Sylvia is responding to. She is disagreeing with Pearl, who said that she and Dan "have nothing in common." Therefore, *kindred* means the opposite of being different. It means "alike, similar."

TEKS 1B

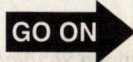
GO ON

45 **Sylvia:** No. Dan is the man for me. Pearl, rubber gloves—
Operation Brunette to Blonde—commence. *(Sylvia pulls out
a bottle of peroxide bleach.)*

*(The two girls disappear into the bathroom as the lights
fade.)*

Scene 4

50 *The Soles' kitchen, dinner that same night*

Mrs. Sole: Guess what, dear. Sylvia got the lead in the
school musical.

Mr. Sole: Was there ever a doubt? She's so talented.

Mrs. Sole: *(shouting)* Sylvia, supper is ready!

55 **Sylvia:** Here I am. *(Sylvia walks into the kitchen. Her hair is
Marilyn Monroe blonde. Her parents stare.)*

Mrs. Sole: Oh, my!

Sylvia: I know. Don't I look great! Today is the debut of the
new and more visible me.

60 **Mr. Sole:** Well, you certainly are visible.

Sylvia: What is that supposed to mean?

Mr. Sole: I was just saying that your hair looks great, but
what makes you stand out is your personality—your inner
qualities, not your appearance.

65 **Sylvia:** We'll see about that.

(Lights fade.)

Scene 5

School the next day

Sylvia: Pearl, guess what! During English, Dan asked me to
sit with him at lunch today. I told you that blondes have more
70 fun!

GO ON

Pearl: Maybe you're right, Sylvia. But I still say he's not your type, even though you want him to be.

(Later that day)

Pearl: Soooo, how was lunch?

75 **Sylvia:** He's a nice guy but . . . *(rolling her eyes)* Every time I tried to talk about books, or the theater, or new movies, he swerved back to sports or his Mustang's sprint engine with an occasional remark thrown in about the tender and tangy turkey fricassee. I should have won an Oscar for my

80 performance. He had no idea how bored I was. You were right, Pearl. I might look different, but I am still the same person inside. I just have to recognize who that person is and start being happy with what makes her unique.

(Lights fade.)

Scene 6

85 *Sylvia's bedroom that evening*

Sylvia: *(lying on her bed, staring at the ceiling)* I can't believe I dyed my hair for a guy! How lame is that!

Mrs. Sole: *(knocking on door)* May I come in?

Sylvia: Hey, Mom.

90 **Mrs. Sole:** Ah, I see you have returned to your original color.

Sylvia: Mom, I am really disappointed in myself for believing that hair color could change who I am. And you're right—I have not been very sweet lately. I think it is time to get over myself. After all, to the people who actually care about me,

95 I am very visible even without a beacon of blonde on my head! Plus, who ever heard of a light-haired Maria in *West Side Story?*

Mrs. Sole: You've learned a lesson that many people never do, which is "To thine own self be true." Of course, you can

100 dye your hair or change the way you dress or talk, but do it for yourself, not for other people. And, Sylvia, I want you to

ELEMENTS OF DRAMA
In her conversation with Pearl, Sylvia shows what she has learned through her experience (lines 81–83). Characters' reactions to events help to bring out the theme, or message, of a work.

TEKS 2A, 4

GO ON ➡

know how proud your father and I are of you for getting the
lead in the school play. You have such a talent, and we
admire the way that you go after your dreams. In fact, we've
105 bought a block of seats for all three nights! We're inviting
everyone we know, and even some we don't!

(Lights fade.)

Scene 7

School the next day

Sylvia: Hi, Mike. Umm, I wondered . . .

110 **Mike:** Hey, Sylvia. It's nice to see the real you again!

Sylvia: Listen, would you want to go to the movies this
weekend?

Mike: I thought you'd never ask!

> **MAKING INFERENCES**
> Notice that in line 110,
> Mike says that he is happy
> to see the "real you" again.
> From this you can infer
> that he was not impressed
> by Sylvia's transformation
> into a blonde.
>
> **Fig. 19B**

Use *Something's Changed* (pp. 28–32) to answer questions 1–6.

1 Read the following dictionary entry.

> **tendency** \tĕn´dən sē\ *n.* **1.** movement in a certain direction **2.** a likelihood **3.** a predisposition to act or think in a certain way **4.** a bias

What is the definition of <u>tendency</u> as it is used in line 26?

A Definition 1
B Definition 2
C Definition 3
D Definition 4

> **EXPLANATION:** Pearl says that Sylvia has a "drama-queen tendency." In other words, she has a habit of acting dramatically in many situations. **C** is correct.
> • **A** is incorrect. This meaning refers to a physical direction rather than an inclination.
> • **B** and **D** are incorrect. Neither meaning fits the context in which the word is used.

TEKS 1B, 1E

2 Which statement about the character of Dan is accurate?

F He serves a mostly symbolic function in the play.
G He is a multi-dimensional character who is central to the action.
H His character is developed through interactions with the others.
J He is a sympathetic character to whom readers can relate.

> **EXPLANATION:** The character of Dan is the reason, or catalyst, for Sylvia's emotional conflict. But he has no dialogue and remains a very one-dimensional figure throughout the play. Therefore, **F** is correct.
> • **G** and **H** are incorrect. Readers learn nothing about the real character of Dan beyond what the other characters say about him. There is no interaction between Dan and anyone else.
> • **J** is incorrect. Although some readers may feel sympathy toward Dan, that is not the primary purpose of his character.

TEKS 4

GO ON ➡

3 When Sylvia's father says in line 60, "Well, you certainly are visible," he means that —

A he approves of her new hair color

B her new hair color is impossible to overlook

C having the lead in the play will make her stand out

D she is the "apple of his eye"

> **EXPLANATION:** Mr. Sole speaks this line in response to Sylvia's comment that she wishes to be visible. He is reacting to her extreme new hair color, implying that there is no way she can be overlooked now. Therefore, **B** is correct.
> - **A** and **D** are incorrect. Sylvia's father's first response is simply to stare, and later he emphasizes that Sylvia's inner qualities are more important than her hair color. His words and actions do not imply approval.
> - **C** is incorrect. Mr. Sole never gets a chance to say anything to Sylvia about her leading role. This comment is in response to her hair color.

TEKS 4; Fig. 19B

4 Which line from the play best expresses its theme?

F *I am getting tired of blending into the scenery.*

G *Of course, you can dye your hair . . . but do it for yourself, not for other people.*

H *Today is the debut of the new and more visible me.*

J *[H]e's not your type, even though you want him to be.*

> **EXPLANATION:** In the course of the play, Sylvia learns the hard way that changing herself to please Dan doesn't work. It only causes her to feel disappointed and unhappy. She realizes that she needs to act in a way that is true to her nature. **G** is correct.
> - **F** is incorrect. This line expresses Sylvia's conflict.
> - **H** is incorrect. Sylvia says this line when she thinks she has resolved her conflict.
> - **J** is incorrect. Although Pearl makes a good point, this is not the main message of the play.

TEKS 2A, 4; Fig. 19B

GO ON

5 Sylvia rolls her eyes in line 75 to express —

   A horror

   B grief

   C impatience

   D disillusionment

> **EXPLANATION:** Sylvia rolls her eyes to emphasize the meaning of her words in this part of the play. She is saying how disappointing her lunch with Dan turned out to be. He was her ideal, but as it turned out, they have nothing in common. **D** is correct.
> - **A** and **B** are incorrect because rolling one's eyes is not a gesture that conveys a strong emotion, such as horror or grief.
> - **C** is incorrect. Although many teenagers roll their eyes to show impatience, in this case Sylvia is not impatient with her friend.

TEKS 4; Fig. 19B

6 Which is an example of an allusion from the play?

   F *beacon of blonde*

   G *tender and tangy turkey fricassee*

   H *"To thine own self be true"*

   J *I've seen mud with better highlights*

> **EXPLANATION: H** is correct. It is a quotation taken from Shakespeare's play *Hamlet.* It is an allusion that reinforces and enriches the meaning of the characters' dialogue.
> - **F** is incorrect. This phrase is a metaphor, comparing the bright blonde hair on Sylvia's head to a beacon or source of light.
> - **G** is incorrect. This phrase is an example of sensory language as well as alliteration, or the repetition of sounds at the beginning of words.
> - **J** is incorrect. This phrase is an example of hyperbole, or exaggeration.

TEKS 7

GO ON

Answer the following question in the space provided.

---

7 Discuss the meaning of the play's title. Explain your answer and support it with evidence from the selection.

EXPLANATION

Rubric, high-scoring response:
- Reflects a perceptive awareness of the text's meaning and complexities; makes meaningful connections across the text
- Uses specific, well-chosen evidence from the text, supporting validity of response
- Shows deep understanding of the text through ideas and supporting text evidence

Sample Response: The title at first appears to refer to Sylvia's hair color. When she returns to her original hue, it would seem as though nothing has changed after all. However, because of her experiences, Sylvia has changed her outlook and has grown. She has a greater awareness of who she is and a realization that she cannot become someone different to please another person. Expressing the play's theme, she exclaims, "I can't believe I dyed my hair for a guy! How lame is that!" She also realizes that her complaint about being invisible is groundless. She is not invisible to those with whom she has a genuine and caring relationship. So, although she is back where she started as far as the change in her appearance, in other ways something fundamental has changed.

TEKS 2A, 4; Fig. 19A, 19B

Reading Informational Text: Expository Text

In this part of the book, you will read a nonfiction book excerpt with instruction about the elements of expository text. Following the selection are sample questions and answers about the excerpt. The purpose of this section is to show you how to understand and analyze expository text.

To begin, review the TEKS that relate to expository text:

EXPOSITORY TEXT TEKS	WHAT IT MEANS TO YOU
(9) Comprehension of Informational Text/Expository Text Students analyze, make inferences and draw conclusions about expository text and provide evidence from text to support their understanding. Students are expected to:	
(A) summarize a text in a manner that captures the author's viewpoint, its main ideas, and its elements without taking a position or expressing an opinion;	You will create a summary that explains the author's viewpoint, includes the main points and elements, and remains objective.
(B) distinguish between inductive and deductive reasoning and analyze the elements of deductively and inductively reasoned texts and the different ways conclusions are supported;	You will tell the difference between inductive and deductive reasoning. You will also analyze the features of deductive and inductive reasoning and the different methods used to support conclusions.
(C) make and defend subtle inferences and complex conclusions about the ideas in text and their organizational patterns; and	You will make sophisticated inferences and conclusions about the ideas and organization of an expository text and defend those inferences and conclusions with evidence from the text.
(D) synthesize ideas and make logical connections (e.g., thematic links, author analyses) between and among multiple texts representing similar or different genres and technical sources and support those findings with textual evidence.	You will synthesize ideas from multiple texts that represent similar or different genres and technical sources and make logical connections between those texts. You will also support your findings with evidence from the texts.

The selection that follows provides instruction on the expository text TEKS as well as other TEKS. It also covers reading comprehension skills, such as summarizing, synthesizing, and making complex inferences about text.

As you read the excerpt from *My First Summer in the Sierra,* notice the author's main idea and the details he provides to support it. The annotations in the margins will guide you as you read.

Guided Reading

Read this selection. Then answer the questions that follow.

from My First Summer in the Sierra

by John Muir

Born in Scotland, John Muir moved to Wisconsin as a boy in 1849. After studying geology and botany in college, Muir walked from Wisconsin to Florida in 1867, observing and sketching plant life along the way. He then sailed to California and explored the Yosemite Valley, surrounded by the Sierra Nevada mountain range. He would later persuade President Theodore Roosevelt to preserve the valley as part of Yosemite National Park. The following selection is from his journal entry on July 1, 1869, when he was employed herding sheep in the mountains.

1 I like to watch the squirrels. There are two species here, the large California gray and the Douglas. The latter is the brightest of all the squirrels I have ever seen, a hot spark of life, making every tree tingle with his prickly toes, a condensed nugget of fresh mountain vigor and valor, as free from disease as a sunbeam. One cannot think of such an animal ever being weary or sick. He seems to think the mountains belong to him, and at first tried to drive away the whole flock of sheep as well as the shepherd and dogs. How he scolds, and what faces he makes, all eyes, teeth, and whiskers! If not so comically small, he would indeed be a dreadful fellow. I should like to know more about his bringing up, his life in the home knot-hole, as well as in the tree-tops, throughout all seasons. Strange that I have not yet found a nest full of young ones. The Douglas is nearly allied to the red squirrel of the Atlantic slope, and may have been distributed to this side of the continent by way of the great unbroken forests of the north.

2 The California gray is one of the most beautiful, and, next to the Douglas, the most interesting of our hairy neighbors. Compared with the Douglas he is twice as large, but far less lively and influential as a worker in the woods, and he manages to make his way through leaves and branches

---

ELEMENTS OF EXPOSITORY TEXT

Expository text is organized to help readers understand the subject. In paragraph 1, Muir clearly states the two types of squirrels he will discuss before supplying details about each. As you read, think about the main ideas and important details you would use to summarize the selection.

TEKS 9A, 9C; Fig. 19A

INDUCTIVE REASONING

Inductive reasoning starts with specific observations, examples, and facts and draws from them a general conclusion or principle. At the end of paragraph 1, Muir uses inductive reasoning to suggest that the Douglas squirrel came to the West Coast from the East Coast. Think about the facts he uses to draw his conclusion.

TEKS 9B; Fig. 19B

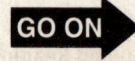
GO ON

with less stir than his small brother. I have never heard him bark at anything except our dogs. When in search of food he glides silently from branch to branch, examining last year's cones, to see whether some few seeds may not be left between the scales, or gleans fallen ones among the leaves on the ground, since none of the present season's crop is yet available. His tail floats now behind him, now above him, level or gracefully curled like a wisp of cirrus cloud, every hair in its place, clean and shining and radiant as thistle-down in spite of rough, gummy work. His whole body seems about as unsubstantial as his tail. The little Douglas is fiery, peppery, full of brag and fight and show, with movements so quick and keen they almost sting the on-looker, and the harlequin gyrating show he makes of himself turns one giddy to see. The gray is shy, and oftentimes stealthy in his movements, as if half expecting an enemy in every tree and bush, and back of every log, wishing only to be let alone apparently, and manifesting no desire to be seen or admired or feared. . . .

SENSORY LANGUAGE
While Muir describes squirrels with a scientist's precision, he also uses beautiful language to help readers picture them. In paragraph 2, he says the Douglas squirrel makes a "harlequin gyrating show" of himself. This sensory language helps readers visualize the movements of a clown or acrobat in a circus. Consider how Muir's vivid style helps him achieve his purpose.

TEKS 7, 8; Fig. 19A

Use the excerpt from *My First Summer in the Sierra* (pp. 38–39) to answer questions 1–6.

1 Read this sentence from paragraph 1.

> *The [Douglas squirrel] is the brightest of all the squirrels I have ever seen, a hot spark of life, making every tree tingle with his prickly toes, a condensed nugget of fresh mountain vigor and valor, as free from disease as a sunbeam.*

What do the imagery and figurative language in this sentence stress about the Douglas squirrel?

A   It is a cute but troublesome creature.

B   It is a large, bumbling creature.

C   It is a lively, vivid creature.

D   It is a healthy but boring creature.

> **EXPLANATION:** Muir describes the Douglas squirrel in language that emphasizes its liveliness, such as "a hot spark of life" and a "nugget of fresh mountain vigor." **C** is correct.
> - **A** is incorrect. None of the details in this sentence suggest that the Douglas squirrel causes any trouble.
> - **B** is incorrect. The phrase "a condensed nugget" suggests that the squirrel is small, and the image of the squirrel "making every tree tingle with his prickly toes" suggests that it is agile, not bumbling.
> - **D** is incorrect. Muir's description of the squirrel as "the brightest of all the squirrels I have ever seen, a hot spark of life" suggests that he considers it to be the opposite of boring.

TEKS 7, 9C; Fig. 19B

2 Study this chart of Muir's inductive reasoning about the Douglas squirrel.

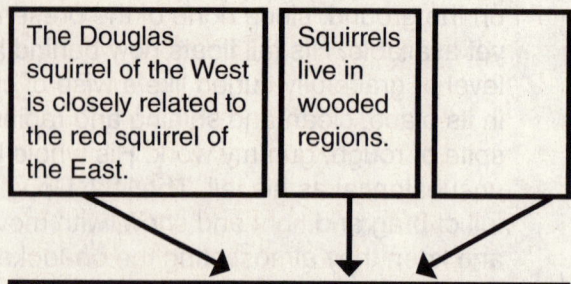

The Douglas squirrel of the West is closely related to the red squirrel of the East.

Squirrels live in wooded regions.

Conclusion: The Douglas squirrel may have come to the West from the East.

Which of the following facts belongs in the empty box to make the conclusion valid?

F   The Douglas squirrel lives in the Sierra Nevada.

G   The red squirrel lives on the Atlantic coast.

H   The Douglas squirrel is livelier than the California gray squirrel.

J   Forests once stretched unbroken from coast to coast.

> **EXPLANATION:** **J** is correct. Since the squirrel lives in wooded regions, or forests, it could only have traveled west through an expanse of forests. At the end of paragraph 1, Muir indicates there was such an expanse when he speaks of "the great unbroken forests of the north."
> - **F** and **G** are incorrect. The chart already contains the fact "The Douglas squirrel of the West is closely related to the red squirrel of the East." Clarifying precisely where each squirrel lives is not the missing detail needed to make the inductive reasoning valid.
> - **H** is incorrect. Although the liveliness of the squirrel might support the idea that it traveled west, it does not provide the essential fact needed to support the conclusion. Without a forested route, the squirrel could not have migrated to the West Coast.

TEKS 9B; Fig. 19B

3 Based on the selection, what seems to be Muir's main purpose in writing this text?

A To persuade readers to visit the Sierra Nevada

B To inform readers about nature in the Sierra

C To explain how species may spread from one part of the country to another

D To entertain readers with amusing images of the Douglas squirrel

> **EXPLANATION:** In the selection, Muir describes two kinds of squirrel found in the Sierra. His writing is full of factual information about the squirrels and the natural landscape they inhabit. **B** is correct.
> - **A** is incorrect. No details in the selection suggest that Muir wants readers to visit the Sierra Nevada. In fact, his descriptions may be most beneficial to readers who will never have the chance to visit.
> - **C** is incorrect. Muir devotes one sentence to his theory of how the Douglas squirrel originally came to the West Coast, but this is not the main purpose of his writing.
> - **D** is incorrect. The text gives equal time to the Douglas squirrel and to the California gray squirrel. Although Muir describes some amusing behaviors of the Douglas squirrel, it is not his main purpose to entertain readers with these details.

TEKS 8; Fig. 19B

4 What is the main or controlling idea of paragraph 2?

F The California gray squirrel, though not as lively as the Douglas squirrel, is still interesting.

G The California gray squirrel is far less interesting than the Douglas squirrel.

H The Douglas squirrel is quick-moving and showy.

J The California gray squirrel has no desire to show off the way the Douglas squirrel does.

> **EXPLANATION: F** is correct. The paragraph's first two sentences express this idea, and it is supported by the details in the rest of the paragraph.
> - **G** is incorrect. The first sentence of the paragraph states that the California gray squirrel *is* interesting, even if it is not quite as interesting as the Douglas squirrel.
> - **H** and **J** are incorrect. Both of these details are included in the paragraph, but they do not express the main idea.

TEKS 9A, 9C; Fig. 19A

5 What is the organizational pattern of the selection as a whole?

A   Comparison and contrast
B   Cause and effect
C   Proposition and support
D   Chronological order

> **EXPLANATION:** Muir begins the selection by introducing two species of squirrel that both live in the Sierra Nevada. In paragraph 1, he provides details about the Douglas squirrel. In paragraph 2, he describes the California gray squirrel, highlighting ways in which it differs from the Douglas squirrel. The last two sentences summarize the contrast between the two squirrels. **A** is correct.
> - **B** is incorrect. Although Muir does speculate about how the Douglas squirrel came west in paragraph 1, his speculation is not the main point of the paragraph or the selection.
> - **C** is incorrect. Although the details in the selection support the idea that the two squirrels are very different, this is not an arguable proposition, and the writing is not structured as an argument.
> - **D** is incorrect. Muir does not narrate events in chronological order.

TEKS 9C

6 Which of the following is the best summary of the selection?

F   While spending a summer in the Sierra Nevada, John Muir encountered two species of squirrel.
G   The lively Douglas squirrel, which may have come to the Sierra from the East Coast, is smaller than the California gray squirrel.
H   Two interesting species of squirrel inhabit the Sierra, the large California gray and the small but lively Douglas.
J   The California gray squirrel is not as active or as interesting as the Douglas squirrel.

> **EXPLANATION:** The correct answer is **H.** It restates the main idea (that there are two interesting species of squirrel in the Sierra); it identifies the two species; and it gives a distinguishing characteristic or detail about each one.
> - **F** is incorrect. It fails to identify the two species of squirrel or tell how they differ. The fact that Muir saw them during a summer in the Sierra is a less important detail.
> - **G** is incorrect. It focuses on the Douglas squirrel and includes a less important detail about how this squirrel may have come to the West.
> - **J** is incorrect. It ignores the first paragraph of the selection, including the main idea. It also states an opinion about the gray squirrel that does not reflect Muir's view.

TEKS 9A; Fig. 19A

Answer the following question in the space provided.

---

7 Think about encyclopedia articles that you encounter when you do research. How does Muir's selection differ from a typical encyclopedia article on squirrels? What, if anything, do the two texts have in common? Support your answer with evidence from the selection.

EXPLANATION
Rubric, high-scoring response:
- Reflects a perceptive awareness of the text's meaning and complexities; makes meaningful connections across the text
- Uses specific, well-chosen evidence from the text, supporting validity of response
- Shows deep understanding of the text through ideas and supporting text evidence

Sample Response: Like an encyclopedia article, the main purpose of this selection is to inform readers about a subject. However, Muir supplies information in a personal and vivid style that an encyclopedia article typically would not use. Muir begins with a personal statement: "I like to watch the squirrels." As he goes on to describe his observations about two species of squirrel, he often includes his own opinions: "The California gray is one of the most beautiful, and, next to the Douglas, the most interesting of our hairy neighbors." Throughout, he uses striking imagery and figurative language to capture the creatures he describes—the Douglas squirrel is "a hot spark of life," "a condensed nugget of fresh mountain vigor and valor," "fiery, peppery, full of brag and fight"; the tail of the California gray squirrel "floats now behind him, now above him, level or gracefully curled like a wisp of cirrus cloud." In contrast, a typical encyclopedia article would provide facts in a formal, objective style and would not include personal experiences or opinions. It would give information about other squirrels to provide a broader context. However, it might not be as interesting to readers because its language would not bring the squirrels to life in the way that Muir's does.

TEKS 7, 8, 9D; Fig. 19A

Reading Informational Text: Persuasive Text

In this part of the book, you will read a persuasive essay with instruction about the elements of persuasive text. Following the selection are sample questions and answers about the essay. The purpose of this section is to show you how to understand and analyze persuasive text.

To begin, review the TEKS that relate to persuasive text:

PERSUASIVE TEXT TEKS	WHAT IT MEANS TO YOU
(10) Comprehension of Informational Text/Persuasive Text Students analyze, make inferences and draw conclusions about persuasive text and provide evidence from text to support their analysis. Students are expected to:	
(A) evaluate how the author's purpose and stated or perceived audience affect the tone of persuasive texts; and	You will evaluate how an author's purpose and audience influence the tone of a persuasive work.
(B) analyze historical and contemporary political debates for such logical fallacies as non-sequiturs, circular logic, and hasty generalizations.	You will analyze whether historical and contemporary debates contain logical fallacies, such as non sequiturs, circular logic, and hasty generalizations.

The selection that follows provides instruction on the persuasive text TEKS as well as other TEKS. It also covers reading comprehension skills, such as making complex inferences about text.

As you read the persuasive essay "School Newspapers Should Be Uncensored," identify the writer's main claim and the evidence used to support it. The annotations in the margins will guide you as you read.

Guided Reading

Read this selection. Then answer the questions that follow.

School Newspapers Should Be Uncensored

1   The Bill of Rights guarantees our right to freedom of the press—unless we happen to be students. More and more principals are currently censoring articles in student newspapers, and the courts are upholding their right to do it.

2   My view is this: as long as the material in a student newspaper is neither obscene nor libelous, its editors and writers should be the only ones who decide its contents. In recent cases, school administrators suppressed articles not for being obscene or libelous but merely for being about controversial subjects that made the administrators uncomfortable. In the famous Hazelwood, Missouri, case and other cases, censored articles were about such topics as divorce, drugs, and gangs. This is not only wrong; it's harmful to students as American citizens. One of the most important life lessons we can learn at school is how to discuss issues in a free society. How can we do this if school administrators won't even let us mention certain issues? Principals who censor these stories aren't "protecting" students from unpleasant issues; they are merely making necessary information harder to get.

3   Student editors and reporters need to know that they can write about what they feel their audience needs to know. If there is a drug problem in their school, for example, they ought to be able to confront it openly. The only thing that's accomplished by not confronting the problem in the school newspaper is that the school newspaper will seem out of touch with reality. Writing about controversial subjects will give students a valuable lesson in freedom and responsibility.

4   Supporters of school administrators' rights of censorship, like Patrick Marshall, think that student reporters have no more right than other reporters to have their stories printed. The censorship, they say, teaches students about the reality of the publishing world, where the publisher holds the power. For example, if a reporter for *The New York Times* wants to write an article on gangs, he can't demand that his publisher print it. The publisher may just not think the subject is newsworthy at the moment.

AUTHOR'S PURPOSE

A persuasive essay often begins with an interesting fact. In paragraph 1, the writer refers to freedom of the press in the Bill of Rights and then states that censorship of student newspapers is a growing trend. These facts give the essay context and introduce the author's purpose, which is to argue against censorship.

TEKS 8, 10

ELEMENTS OF PERSUASIVE TEXT

In paragraph 2, the writer states a strong position and then provides evidence to support it. Supporting evidence may include specific facts, examples, or quotations. Here, the writer provides an example of one type of censorship and explains why it is harmful.

TEKS 10

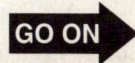
GO ON

5   My reply is, should school newspapers follow the same corporate pattern? Do student journalists sign up for this difficult and rewarding extracurricular activity in order to learn how to knuckle under to higher-ups? When we're adults, will we be more professional newspaper reporters, more powerful thinkers, and more responsible Americans because of our experience hearing the principal tell us, "You can't write that"?

6   Learning the value of freedom of speech and press is more important than learning what power corporate heads sometimes have. It's exactly the kind of lesson that parents pay the schools to teach their children. We learn about it in social studies. We should be allowed to practice it in real life.

7   Mr. Marshall and others want to teach students that power belongs to the people who own newspapers. My position is that we, the students and our parents, are the ones who own the school newspaper. It is funded with tax money or tuition. The principal has no financial investment in the school paper; therefore he or she is not its publisher. By Patrick Marshall's own logic, we deserve the power to control our newspaper's contents. Administrators should have a great deal of control over what is taught in their schools, but not over what students can decently say. The first journalism lesson students must learn is that they can have the power to express themselves freely.

TONE
A writer may try to match his or her tone, or attitude, to the audience's. In paragraph 5, the writer responds to the argument that, in the real world, a corporate publisher can refuse to print a story for a variety of reasons. Read the writer's response carefully and think about the tone conveyed by the choice of words.

TEKS 10A

ELEMENTS OF PERSUASIVE TEXT
In paragraph 7, the writer connects facts presented in the essay to draw a final conclusion and restate the main argument. The writer concludes that students are the actual owners of their school newspapers and, as the owners, they should have the power to express themselves as they see fit.

TEKS 10; Fig. 19A

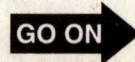
GO ON

Use "School Newspapers Should Be Uncensored" (pp. 45–46) to answer questions 1–7.

1 Which of the following statements best describes the main argument of the selection?

A Most principals and superintendents do not understand the purpose of a newspaper.

B Students should have the freedom to express themselves without being censored.

C Some schools censor articles about divorce, drugs, and gangs.

D Many students want to write about topics that make adults uncomfortable.

EXPLANATION: This question asks you to identify the main argument the writer makes in the persuasive essay. **B** is correct because it accurately states the writer's position on the censorship of school newspapers.

- **A** is incorrect. The writer never states that most principals and superintendents do not understand the purpose of a newspaper.
- **C** is incorrect. This is one fact presented in the essay, not the main idea.
- **D** is incorrect. The writer does not believe the goal of student journalists is to make adults uncomfortable. They want to write about topics that are meaningful to them.

TEKS 8, 10; Fig. 19B

2 Which sentence from the selection states a reason to keep school newspapers uncensored?

F *Supporters of school administrators' rights of censorship, like Patrick Marshall, think that student reporters have no more right than other reporters to have their stories printed.*

G *Writing about controversial subjects will give students a valuable lesson in freedom and responsibility.*

H *More and more principals are currently censoring articles in student newspapers, and the courts are upholding their right to do it.*

J *Do student journalists sign up for this difficult and rewarding extracurricular activity in order to learn how to knuckle under to higher-ups?*

EXPLANATION: G is correct because it points out the importance of giving students the freedom to think and write about controversial topics. This is a reason for keeping school newspapers uncensored.

- **F** is incorrect. It states an opposing position held by people who feel school newspapers should be censored.
- **H** is incorrect. It is a fact related to student censorship, but it does not support the argument that students should be uncensored.
- **J** is incorrect. This rhetorical question is part of an argument against censorship, but it is not a stated reason to oppose censorship.

TEKS 10

3 Which of the following is evidence supporting the claim that school administrators censor articles that make them uncomfortable?

A Publishers sometimes reject articles they feel are not newsworthy.

B Some principals believe students don't have the right to have all stories printed.

C School newspapers that do not address real problems might seem out of touch with reality.

D In one famous case, censored articles were about divorce, drugs, and gangs.

EXPLANATION: In paragraph 2, the writer says, "In recent cases, school administrators suppressed articles . . . merely for being about controversial subjects that made the administrators uncomfortable." The writer then supports this statement by citing the specific case in Hazelwood, Missouri, in which articles about divorce, drugs, and gangs were censored. **D** is correct.

- **A** is incorrect. This is a fact presented to support an opposing argument in support of censorship.
- **B** is incorrect. Although this general idea helps establish the context for the article, it is not presented as supporting evidence.
- **C** is incorrect. This is an opinion expressed by the writer and is not supporting evidence.

TEKS 10

4 Which statement best describes the writer's counterargument to the opinion that students should be censored because censorship is a fact of life in the publishing world?

F The United States Bill of Rights guarantees free speech.

G Students want to write about controversial topics.

H Students are not yet in the corporate world and need experience exploring a variety of ideas and topics.

J Students should have an experience similar to that of real-world reporters, who can print articles on any topic they want.

EXPLANATION: In paragraph 4, the writer outlines an opposing argument: that censorship of school newspapers is acceptable because it's similar to the editorial decisions made by publishers in the corporate world. The writer's response is that school is different from the corporate world and should give students the opportunity to express themselves freely. **H** is correct.

- **F** is incorrect. Although it is a fact presented in the selection, it is not used as a counterargument.
- **G** is incorrect. This is not mentioned as a counterargument.
- **J** is incorrect. The selection states that reporters are in fact sometimes censored by their publishers.

TEKS 10

5 According to the writer of the essay, principals do not have the right to censor students because —

A reporters in the real world are never censored or restricted in any way

B many principals do not have experience working for real newspapers

C principals are too busy to spend time reading student writing

D students and their parents, as taxpayers, actually own the school newspaper

EXPLANATION: In paragraph 7, the writer states that students and parents own the school newspaper because they pay taxes and tuition. **D** is correct.
- **A** is incorrect. The writer acknowledges that reporters in the real world are sometimes told what they can and cannot print by their publishers.
- **B** and **C** are incorrect. Neither of these ideas is mentioned in the essay.

TEKS 10

6 Read this passage from the essay.

My reply is, should school newspapers follow the same corporate pattern? Do student journalists sign up for this difficult and rewarding extracurricular activity in order to learn how to knuckle under to higher-ups?

What attitude is conveyed by the phrase "learn how to knuckle under to higher-ups," and what does the writer probably assume about the audience?

F It conveys a tone of admiration for corporate discipline, but the writer assumes the audience disagrees with this attitude.

G It conveys a tone of scorn toward some aspects of corporate culture, and the writer assumes the audience is sympathetic to this attitude.

H It conveys a tone of disapproval toward corporate practices, but the writer assumes the audience would favor making school activities more like the corporate world.

J It conveys a neutral tone toward corporate power structures, and the writer assumes the audience has the same neutral attitude.

EXPLANATION: The expression *knuckle under* has negative connotations; it implies weakness or giving up instead of fighting for something important. **G** is correct because the passage expresses scorn for the idea that powerful people should get to make all the decisions. The writer assumes the audience has similar feelings, making them more sympathetic to the argument against censorship in school.
- **F** and **J** are incorrect. The writer's language expresses a negative attitude, not a positive or a neutral one.
- **H** is incorrect. If the audience seemed to favor making school more like the corporate world, the writer would not use negative language about corporate practices for fear of offending them.

TEKS 10A

GO ON ➡

7 According to the author, which of the following is an example of faulty reasoning?

A School administrators are publishers and therefore have the right to censor articles.

B Students should be able to practice the principles of free speech that they are taught in school.

C Students are too immature to deal sensitively with controversial issues.

D A school newspaper's failure to deal with controversial issues will make it seem irrelevant.

EXPLANATION: The writer says in paragraph 7 that Patrick Marshall believes a newspaper's owners should control its contents. The writer goes on to say that because students and parents actually own school newspapers, they should control content. He thus points out the flaw in Marshall's logic that administrators have the right to censor content. **A** is correct.

- **B** and **D** are incorrect. These are the writer's own arguments and they are well supported.
- **C** is incorrect. Although it does represent an overgeneralization, this counterargument is not presented in the essay.

TEKS 10B

Name _____ Date _____

Answer the following question in the space provided.

---

8 Does the writer of "School Newspapers Should Be Uncensored" make a strong and persuasive argument? Explain why you do or do not agree with the evidence and ideas presented. Support your answer with evidence from the selection.

EXPLANATION

Rubric, high-scoring response:
- Reflects a perceptive awareness of the text's meaning and complexities; makes meaningful connections across the text
- Uses specific, well-chosen evidence from the text, supporting validity of response
- Shows deep understanding of the text through ideas and supporting text evidence

Sample Response: In "School Newspapers Should Be Uncensored," the writer claims that student reporters should be allowed to write about a variety of topics, even controversial topics, without being censored by school administrators. I believe the writer makes a strong argument. The writer explains that in some cases, censored articles concern topics that are very important to students, even though they make administrators uncomfortable. The writer feels this censorship is wrong: "Principals who censor these stories aren't 'protecting' students from unpleasant issues; they are merely making necessary information harder to get." The writer addresses the argument that, in the real world, reporters cannot always write what they want because publishers control what is printed. However, I agree with the writer's counterargument that students must learn how to think about different topics and express themselves freely. I also agree with the statement that students, not administrators, own school newspapers and should be responsible for the content of those newspapers.

TEKS 10; Fig. 19A

Reading Informational Text: Paired Selections

In this part of the book, you will read two selections: a speech with instruction about the elements of persuasive text and an informational article with instruction about the elements of expository text. Following the selections are sample questions and answers about the two pieces. The purpose of this section is to show you how to understand and analyze selections from two different genres and how to compare and contrast them.

To begin, review the TEKS that relate to persuasive and expository text:

PERSUASIVE TEXT TEKS	WHAT IT MEANS TO YOU
(10) Comprehension of Informational Text/Persuasive Text Students analyze, make inferences and draw conclusions about persuasive text and provide evidence from text to support their analysis. Students are expected to:	
(A) evaluate how the author's purpose and stated or perceived audience affect the tone of persuasive texts; and	You will evaluate how an author's purpose and audience influence the tone of a persuasive work.
(B) analyze historical and contemporary political debates for such logical fallacies as non-sequiturs, circular logic, and hasty generalizations.	You will analyze whether historical and contemporary debates contain logical fallacies, such as non sequiturs, circular logic, and hasty generalizations.

EXPOSITORY TEXT TEKS	WHAT IT MEANS TO YOU
(9) Comprehension of Informational Text/Expository Text Students analyze, make inferences and draw conclusions about expository text and provide evidence from text to support their understanding. Students are expected to:	
(A) summarize a text in a manner that captures the author's viewpoint, its main ideas, and its elements without taking a position or expressing an opinion;	You will create a summary that explains the author's viewpoint, includes the main points and elements, and remains objective.
(B) distinguish between inductive and deductive reasoning and analyze the elements of deductively and inductively reasoned texts and the different ways conclusions are supported;	You will tell the difference between inductive and deductive reasoning. You will also analyze the features of deductive and inductive reasoning and the different methods used to support conclusions.
(C) make and defend subtle inferences and complex conclusions about the ideas in text and their organizational patterns; and	You will make sophisticated inferences and conclusions about the ideas and organization of an expository text and defend those inferences and conclusions with evidence from the text.
(D) synthesize ideas and make logical connections (e.g., thematic links, author analyses) between and among multiple texts representing similar or different genres and technical sources and support those findings with textual evidence.	You will synthesize ideas from multiple texts that represent similar or different genres and technical sources and make logical connections between those texts. You will also support your findings with evidence from the texts.

The selections that follow provide instruction on the persuasive and expository text TEKS as well as other TEKS. They also cover reading comprehension skills, such as summarizing, synthesizing, and making inferences about text.

As you read the speech "The Pleasure of Books" and the informational article "The Future of the Book: Printed or Electronic?" notice how the authors use the elements described in the charts on page 52. Notice also the similarities and differences in structure and meaning between the speech and the article. The annotations in the margins will guide you as you read.

Guided Reading

Read the next two selections. Then answer the questions that follow.

The Pleasure of Books

by William Lyon Phelps

William Lyon Phelps, a Yale University English professor for over thirty years, delivered this speech as a radio broadcast in 1933.

1   The habit of reading is one of the greatest resources of mankind; and we enjoy reading books that belong to us much more than if they are borrowed. A borrowed book is like a guest in the house; it must be treated with punctiliousness, with a certain considerate formality. You must see that it sustains no damage; it must not suffer while under your roof. You cannot leave it carelessly, you cannot mark it, you cannot turn down the pages, you cannot use it familiarly. And then, some day, although this is seldom done, you really ought to return it.

2   But your own books belong to you; you treat them with that affectionate intimacy that annihilates[1] formality. Books are for use, not for show; you should own no book that you are afraid to mark up, or afraid to place on the table, wide open and face down. A good reason for marking favorite passages in books is that this practice enables you to remember more easily the significant sayings, to refer to them quickly, and then in later years, it is like visiting a forest where you once blazed a trail. You have the pleasure of going over the old ground, and recalling both the intellectual scenery and your own earlier self.

3   Everyone should begin collecting a private library in youth; the instinct of private property, which is fundamental in human beings, can here be cultivated with every advantage and no evils. One should have one's own bookshelves, which should not have doors, glass windows, or keys; they should be free and accessible to the hand as well as to the eye. The best of mural decorations is books; they are more varied in color and appearance than any wallpaper, they are more

CONTEXT CLUES
When you see an unfamiliar word, look for words and phrases around it that may state the same meaning in a different way. In paragraph 1, the phrase "with a certain considerate formality" tells you that *punctiliousness* means "strict care."

TEKS 1B

LOGICAL FALLACIES
When reading a persuasive text, be alert for fallacies, or errors in reasoning, such as the overgeneralization in paragraph 2. This statement expresses the speaker's strong feelings but is too broad to be valid.

TEKS 10B

ELEMENTS OF PERSUASIVE TEXT
Note that the speaker does not state his claim, or position, until paragraph 3. The first two paragraphs introduce the importance of book ownership and provide context for the claim.

TEKS 10A

---

1. **annihilates:** destroys.

GO ON ➡

attractive in design, and they have the prime advantage of being separate personalities, so that if you sit alone in the room in the firelight, you are surrounded with intimate friends. The knowledge that they are there in plain view is both stimulating and refreshing. You do not have to read them all. Most of my indoor life is spent in a room containing six thousand books; and I have a <u>stock</u> answer to the invariable question that comes from strangers. "Have you read all of these books?" "Some of them twice." This reply is both true and unexpected.

4   There are of course no friends like living, breathing, corporeal[2] men and women; my devotion to reading has never made me a recluse.[3] How could it? Books are of the people, by the people, for the people. Literature is the immortal part of history; it is the best and most enduring part of personality. But book-friends have this advantage over living friends; you can enjoy the most truly aristocratic[4] society in the world whenever you want it. The great dead are beyond our physical reach, and the great living are usually almost as inaccessible; as for our personal friends and acquaintances, we cannot always see them. Perchance they are asleep, or away on a journey. But in a private library, you can at any moment converse with Socrates or Shakespeare or Carlyle or Dumas or Dickens or Shaw or Barrie or Galsworthy. And there is no doubt that in these books you see these men at their best. They wrote for *you.* They "laid themselves out," they did their ultimate best to entertain you, to make a favorable impression. You are necessary to them as an audience is to an actor; only instead of seeing them masked, you look into their innermost heart of hearts.

ELEMENTS OF PERSUASIVE TEXT
The speaker assumes his audience will recognize his allusion to Lincoln's Gettysburg Address in paragraph 4. He uses Lincoln's phrasing to reinforce his central idea.

TEKS 10A

TONE
The speaker's choice of words and details reveals his tone, or attitude toward his subject. Consider how the use of *perchance,* "perhaps," in paragraph 4 contributes to your understanding of the speaker's tone.

TEKS 10A

---

2. **corporeal:** real; physically present.
3. **recluse:** someone who lives apart from others and prefers not to socialize with anyone.
4. **aristocratic:** noble or high-ranking.

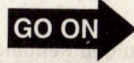
GO ON

The Future of the Book: Printed or Electronic?

1   Imagine this: You are rummaging through some odds and ends at an antique store, and you come across an old printed book. The pages are yellowed and the paper cover is torn. It is William Shakespeare's *Macbeth,* a play you read last year for English class after downloading the complete works of Shakespeare onto your PDA. You squint at the artifact in your hand, which has tiny print and is cluttered with confusing footnotes and annotations on every page. Long ago, someone scrawled notes in the margin and even doodled a bit. You have never seen one of these before, although your parents have mentioned them. Why on earth did anyone ever like these things? You shrug and toss it back onto the pile.

2   Is this the future? Will printed books become extinct as more e-books become available? Many people think so, for new electronic technology continues to make reading more convenient and less expensive.

How Are E-books and Printed Books Different?

3   Printed and electronic books are distant cousins. You can flip through a printed book, front to back, or turn each page slowly, enjoying the texture of the pages. You can lay it face down on a table while you go do something else. You can place it on a bookshelf next to its fellows.

4   An e-book is different. You can't touch the pages. But you can very quickly search the entire text for words, phrases, or specific information—this is not easy to do with a printed book. E-readers are easy on the eyes: you can shrink or enlarge the text as you need to. You can also easily create notes and call them up. E-books may cost less than most printed books, and they are easy to download. Most of all, e-books—light and compact—offer convenience. You can carry them with you on portable e-readers or download them onto your computer. People who travel can carry thousands of books with them, instead of being limited to the few they can cram into a suitcase. What reader wouldn't want to set printed books aside and pick up these wonderful things?

CONTEXT CLUES

Writers choose words for their connotations as well as for their dictionary definitions. In paragraph 1, *artifact,* which means "an ancient object or relic," has the connotation of "outdated" or "not very useful."

TEKS 1B

INDUCTIVE REASONING

The writer presents a conclusion about e-books in paragraph 2. Look for facts in the next paragraphs that support this inductive reasoning, or reasoning from specific facts and examples to a general conclusion.

TEKS 9B, 9C; Fig. 19B

ELEMENTS OF EXPOSITORY TEXT

The facts in paragraph 4 lead to the conclusion that e-books are convenient. Notice the frequent use of the word *easy* in describing the e-book's features.

TEKS 9B, 9C

GO ON

The E-book Revolution

5   Today, e-books in the public domain—books whose copyrights have expired—number in the millions. Anyone with an e-reader or a computer can download these titles for free. Millions of other e-books are sold by publishers, bookstores and book warehouses, and by the authors themselves.

6   The e-book was invented in 1971, when a college student named Michael Hart began to think that literary works in the public domain should be available to everyone for no cost. He and a few volunteers began to create text files of these works by typing them in. They spent the next several years typing in books such as the Bible and the collected works of Shakespeare. Project Gutenberg, as it came to be known, completed its tenth e-book in 1989. By the early part of this century, Project Gutenberg offered more than 33,000 free titles online, and digital libraries around the world have followed its lead, making Hart's dream a reality.

7   In addition to public domain titles, these libraries offer a variety of materials. Students and researchers have access to an enormous amount of online content, in all languages. Archives from subjects as varied as medieval military history, Finnish literature, and archery can be explored and materials either downloaded or viewed online. Many periodicals and their archives are available, too, as are thousands of pages of sheet music and audio files.

E-books in Schools

8   The e-book revolution has certainly transformed the way readers can gain access to entertainment and information, but how has it influenced education? Textbooks, as any college student will tell you, are simply too expensive. At Daytona State College in Ohio, for example, students struggled with textbook costs that were a huge part of their overall expenses. In response, in 2011 the school decided to have all students buy e-books. Publishers sold the school a license, which gave students access to these books. The school charged each student a "digital materials" fee. This fee was much lower than the cost of a new print textbook.

MAKING INFERENCES
A writer's choice of details often reveals his or her purpose. Think about why the writer chooses to include the history of the e-book in paragraph 6.

TEKS 8, 9C; Fig. 19B

ELEMENTS OF EXPOSITORY TEXT
Paragraph 8 provides a specific example of how e-books can be less expensive than traditional print books. This adds support for the conclusion identified in paragraph 2.

TEKS 9B, 9C

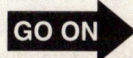

9 How did students feel about this transition? Many seemed to like the new plan, but others were initially uncomfortable reading all the materials on a computer screen or a portable e-reader. Students were not forced to use e-books if they didn't want to. They could print out the books and put the pages in a three-ring binder if they preferred that format.

10 Other schools around the country have established pilot programs to determine the effectiveness and cost advantage of e-books over the print versions. Whether or not e-books completely replace print textbooks at most colleges and universities remains to be seen.

What Does the Future Hold?

11 As e-books become more widely available, the future of the traditional printed book is uncertain. Many books (including textbooks) are still published in both print and digital versions. More and more, however, the trend is toward the digital format. The advantages of the electronic technology are inarguable. E-readers make books easier and cheaper to acquire and read. People have access to millions of free titles, and they can buy new titles for much lower prices than are charged for printed books. Students can save money, and schools can provide a wider variety of reference materials for their students. In an interview, Michael Hart said, "I don't see how paper can possibly compete once people find their own comfortable way to e-texts, especially in schools."

12 Most e-books are made of plastic—a cold and hard material. They do not feel or look or smell like printed books. Some lovers of printed books may be unhappy as the technology continues to evolve. But who knows? Perhaps even they will come to like e-books, and they will set their printed books aside—or put them in the basement, where future generations may discover them and sell them as antiques.

> **ELEMENTS OF EXPOSITORY TEXT**
> In paragraph 11, the writer incorporates a quotation from Michael Hart, who pioneered e-books. Think about how this expert opinion affects your perception of what you have read.
>
> **TEKS 9C; Fig. 19A**

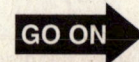

Use "The Pleasure of Books" (pp. 54–55) to answer questions 1–6.

---

1 What is the tone of this speech?

A Formally conversational

B Informally enthusiastic

C Reflective and reserved

D Offhand and casual

EXPLANATION: The style of this speech includes challenging vocabulary and complex sentences, resulting in a formal tone. Yet the formality is balanced by the speaker's use of the pronoun *you,* which gives listeners the feeling that he is talking directly to them. **A** is correct.
- **B** is incorrect. The word choice is anything but informal.
- **C** is incorrect. While the tone may be described as reflective, the speaker feels too strongly about his subject to be called reserved.
- **D** is incorrect. The speaker is involved with his subject, not offhand, and is formal, rather than casual.

TEKS 10A

2 Which statement from the speech is an example of a logical fallacy?

F *And then, some day, although this is seldom done, you really ought to return it.*

G *[T]hey have the prime advantage of being separate personalities. . . .*

H *Literature is the immortal part of history. . . .*

J *[W]e enjoy reading books that belong to us much more than if they are borrowed.*

EXPLANATION: A logical fallacy is often based on an incorrect inference or a misuse of evidence. **J** is correct. The statement is an overgeneralization. Because the speaker feels this way, he generalizes this feeling to include everyone.
- **F, G,** and **H** are incorrect. These statements show no error in reasoning but rather present the speaker's view or observations.

TEKS 10B

GO ON

3 Which of the following best identifies the speaker's purpose?

A To compare and contrast borrowed books with books that someone owns

B To urge his audience to read more

C To argue that schools should make books more accessible to their students

D To persuade his audience that owning books will enrich their lives

EXPLANATION: The details throughout the speech reveal the purpose to be convincing listeners that owning their own books will enrich their lives. In paragraph 3, he claims, "Everyone should begin collecting a private library in youth." He later says that "in a private library, you can at any moment converse with Socrates or Shakespeare." **D** is correct.

- **A** is incorrect. He does compare and contrast borrowed books with those that someone owns, but only to introduce the idea of ownership.
- **B** is incorrect. Although the speaker would likely want his audience to read more, that is not his primary reason for speaking.
- **C** is incorrect. No details support this interpretation of the speaker's purpose.

TEKS 8, 10A; Fig. 19B

4 In paragraph 2, the speaker says that "you treat [books that you own] with that affectionate intimacy that annihilates formality." Which of the following is an accurate paraphrase of this statement?

F Owned books can be handled with familiarity and ease.

G People treat their own books better than borrowed books.

H Owned books are soon destroyed.

J You should not worry about taking care of your own books.

EXPLANATION: This question asks you to put the speaker's words into your own words. *Affectionate, intimacy, annihilates,* and *formality* are the key words that convey the meaning that one's own books can be handled as if they are old friends with whom one is comfortable. **F** is correct.

- **G, H,** and **J** are incorrect. They may be true, but they are not accurate paraphrases of the quoted text.

Fig. 19A

5 What does the speaker's frequent use of comparisons to common experiences—such as "a borrowed book is like a guest in the house" and "it is like visiting a forest where you once blazed a trail"—suggest about his audience?

A He is speaking to a select group of book specialists and librarians.

B He is addressing other university professors.

C He is directing his ideas to a broad and diverse audience.

D He is presenting a lecture to his graduate students in literature.

EXPLANATION: The comparisons that the speaker makes as well as some of his examples are fairly straightforward and simple. This element of his style suggests that he wants all of his listeners to understand what he is saying, and that he has a broader audience than just members of his own profession or class. **C** is correct.

- **A, B,** and **D** are incorrect. The speaker's comparisons would most likely be more literary if he were talking just to his colleagues, advanced students, or others in fields closely related to his.

TEKS 10A

6 In paragraph 3, the word <u>stock</u> means —

F original

G routine

H varied

J quick

EXPLANATION: The context says that the speaker gives a stock reply to "the invariable question that comes from strangers"—a question he has heard many times and has come to expect. This suggests that it is a reply he gives without having to think about it, or one that he gives routinely. **G** is correct.

- **F** is incorrect. This is the opposite of what the context suggests.
- **H** is incorrect. The speaker would not be able to quote just one reply if he changed his response each time.
- **J** is incorrect. He may respond quickly, but only because his answer is standard or routine enough that he doesn't have to think about it.

TEKS 1B

GO ON

Use "The Future of the Book: Printed or Electronic?" (pp. 56–58) to answer questions 7–10.

7 Which of these phrases conveys the intended meaning of <u>squint</u> in paragraph 1?

  A To look at with difficulty

  B To look at closely

  C To look at with interest

  D To look at briefly

> **EXPLANATION:** The words and phrases in the paragraph—such as "tiny print," "cluttered," and "confusing footnotes"—all suggest that the book is hard to read. Therefore, *squint* in this context has the connotation of being difficult. **A** is correct.
> - **B** is incorrect. In another context, this meaning might be accurate, but in this context the writer obviously wants to show how hard it is to read old printed books.
> - **C** and **D** are incorrect. Neither meaning is supported by the context.

TEKS 1B

8 Which of these is an accurate summary of the selection?

  F Unlike printed books, electronic books are compact. Millions can be accessed from a small electronic reader or computer. They are great for travelers and students.

  G The electronic book movement started in 1971 and has grown since then. Now, not only public domain texts are available but millions of other books as well. E-books have transformed the way books are published.

  H Electronic books are more convenient and less expensive than printed books. They provide easy access to millions of books that can be read comfortably using a small reader. Many e-books are free, and others can be purchased for a low price.

  J E-books are far superior to printed books and are quickly making the latter obsolete. Printed books are cumbersome, hard to read, and expensive. E-books are compact, easy to read, and relatively cheap. There is no comparison between the two.

> **EXPLANATION:** A summary includes the main ideas and the most important details of a selection. The main idea is that e-books are more convenient and less expensive than printed books. **H** is correct.
> - **F** is incorrect. This statement does not cover all of the main ideas of the selection.
> - **G** is incorrect. This summary focuses mostly on the section entitled "The E-book Revolution."
> - **J** is incorrect. It includes several opinions rather than an objective restating of main ideas.

TEKS 9A; Fig. 19A

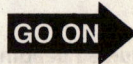 GO ON

9 Which statement from the selection is a valid conclusion drawn from the facts and other details presented?

    A *E-readers are easy on the eyes. . . .*

    B *They do not feel or look or smell like printed books.*

    C *[T]he trend is toward the digital format.*

    D *[S]chools can provide a wider variety of reference materials for their students.*

> **EXPLANATION:** This question asks you to draw a conclusion through inductive reasoning—that is, based on the facts in the selection. Many of the facts support the ideas that digital technology is here to stay and that e-books seem likely to replace printed books, at least for certain purposes. **C** is correct.
> - **A** and **B** are incorrect. They are observations about e-books, not conclusions based on an accumulation of facts.
> - **D** is incorrect. It is a fact rather than a conclusion.

TEKS 9B, 9C; Fig. 19B

10 What is the writer's purpose in this selection?

    F To explain the advantages of e-books

    G To persuade readers to buy e-books

    H To share facts about the technology behind electronic books and readers

    J To narrate a personal experience that shows the value of e-books

> **EXPLANATION:** The details and language that a writer uses reveal his or her purpose. In this selection, the writer presents many facts about the positive aspects of electronic books and the reasons for their increasing popularity. Therefore, **F** is correct. The writer's primary purpose is to explain or inform.
> - **G** is incorrect. Although the writer's evidence could be used in an argument for buying e-books, she does not make that argument herself.
> - **H** is incorrect. The details that the writer includes are not related to the way electronic books work.
> - **J** is incorrect. The writer does not include any details about a personal experience.

TEKS 8, 9C; Fig. 19B

Use "The Pleasure of Books" and "The Future of the Book" (pp. 54–58) to answer questions 11–12.

11 Unlike Phelps, the writer of the expository selection appears to value books primarily for —

A the pleasure of owning them
B their pleasant company
C the challenge of collecting them
D their content

> **EXPLANATION:** This question asks you to focus on the different reasons why Phelps and the writer of the second selection value books. Throughout the second selection, the writer's emphasis is on the quantity and range of information that can be accessed through e-books, making **D** correct. This writer values what the books say and has no need to possess physical copies of them.
> • **A** is incorrect. Although books are saved on an e-reader or computer, the writer of the second selection makes no reference to this feature, indicating that owning books means little.
> • **B** is incorrect. This sense of books as personalities and thus friends or companions is brought out by Phelps but not by the writer of the expository selection.
> • **C** is incorrect. E-books eliminate any process of collecting. They are either available in digital format or not.

TEKS 9D; Fig. 19A, 19B

12 What might Phelps appreciate about electronic books?

F Their use of the latest technology
G Their lack of a physical dimension
H Having access to millions of books
J The streamlined design of modern e-readers

> **EXPLANATION:** In his speech, Phelps urges everyone to collect a library, suggesting that he believes that everyone should have many books. From this, you might infer that he would approve of the way electronic books offer broad, instant access to the great authors and great works. **H** is correct.
> • **F** is incorrect. It is not clear how Phelps views technology. No accurate inference can be made based on the details in the speech.
> • **G** and **J** are incorrect. Phelps loves the look and variety of books, calling them the "best of mural decorations." He would likely find the e-reader unsatisfying aesthetically and would miss what he truly delights in, the books themselves.

TEKS 9D; Fig. 19B

GO ON

Answer the following question in the space provided.

---

13 Do Phelps and the writer of the second selection have anything in common? Explain. Support your answer with evidence from **both** selections.

EXPLANATION

Rubric, high-scoring response:
- Reflects a perceptive awareness of the texts' meaning and complexities; makes meaningful connections across the texts
- Uses specific, well-chosen evidence from the texts, supporting validity of response
- Shows deep understanding of the texts through ideas and supporting text evidence

Sample Response: Both the speaker and the writer are excited about books, whether print or electronic. Phelps calls them "intimate friends" and advocates starting a private library at a young age in order to fully appreciate the experience of owning many volumes. The writer thinks that e-books are "wonderful things" and sees them as opening up new worlds for students and researchers, who have "access to an enormous amount of online content, in all languages." Phelps is also awed by the fact that he can "at any moment converse" with one of the great authors by turning to a volume in his private library. Similarly, the writer of the second selection is awed by the vastness of the electronic network that can put Finnish literature, sheet music, and other obscure materials at anyone's fingertips.

TEKS 9D; Fig. 19A

Reading Practice

Reading Practice

> **Read this selection. Then answer the questions that follow.**

Ginger for the Heart

by Paul Yee

My notes about
what I am reading

*Nearly all the Chinese immigrants to North America in the early
years of the 20th century could tell tales of loved ones left
behind. Here is one such story. Its author, Paul Yee, grew up in the
Chinatown district of Vancouver, on Canada's Pacific coast.*

1   The buildings of Chinatown are stoutly constructed of
brick, and while some are broad and others thin, they rise no
higher than four solid storeys. Many contain stained-glass
windows decorated with flower and diamond patterns, and
others boast balconies with fancy wrought-iron railings.

2   Only one building stands above the rest. Its turret-like
tower is visible even from the harbor, because the cone-
shaped roof is made of copper.

3   In the early days, Chang the merchant tailor owned this
building. He used the main floor for his store and rented out
the others. But he kept the tower room for his own use, for
the sun filled it with light. This was the room where his wife
and daughter worked.

4   His daughter's name was Yenna, and her beauty was
beyond compare. She had ivory skin, sparkling eyes, and
her hair hung long and silken, shining like polished ebony.[1]
All day long she and her mother sat by the tower window
and sewed with silver needles and silken threads. They sang
songs while they worked, and their voices rose in wondrous
harmonies.

5   In all Chinatown, the craftsmanship of Yenna and her
mother was considered the finest. Search as they might,
customers could not discern where holes had once pierced
their shirts. Buttonholes never stretched out of shape, and
seams were all but invisible.

---

1. **ebony:** a dark-colored wood often used for the black keys on a piano keyboard.

GO ON ➡

My notes about
what I am reading

6   One day, a young man came into the store laden with garments for mending. His shoulders were broad and strong, yet his eyes were soft and caring. Many times he came, and many times he saw Yenna. For hours he would sit and watch her work. They fell deeply in love, though few words were spoken between them.

7   Spring came and boats bound for the northern gold fields began to sail again. It was time for the young man to go. He had borrowed money to pay his way over to the New World, and now he had to repay his debts. Onto his back he threw his blankets and tools, food and warm jackets. Then he set off with miners from around the world, clutching gold pans and shovels.

8   Yenna had little to give him in farewell. All she found in the kitchen was a ginger root as large as her hand. As she stroked its brown knobs and bumpy eyes, she whispered to him, "This will warm you in the cold weather. I will wait for you, but, like this piece of ginger, I, too, will age and grow dry." Then she pressed her lips to the ginger, and turned away.

9   "I will come back," the young man said. "The fire burning for you in my heart can never be extinguished."

10   Thereafter, Yenna lit a lamp at every nightfall and set it in the tower window. Rains lashed against the glass, snow piled low along the ledge, and ocean winds rattled the frame. But the flame did not waver, even though the young man never sent letters. Yenna did not weep uselessly, but continued to sew and sing with her mother.

11   There were few unmarried women in Chinatown, and many men came to seek Yenna's hand in marriage. Rich gold miners and sons of successful merchants bowed before her, but she always looked away. They gave her grand gifts, but still she shook her head, until finally the men grew weary and called her crazy. In China, parents arranged all marriages, and daughters became the property of their husbands. But Chang the merchant tailor treasured his daughter's happiness and let her be.

12   One winter, an epidemic ravaged the city. When it was over, Chang had lost his wife and his eyesight. Yenna led him up to the tower where he could feel the sun and drifting

clouds move across his face. She began to sew again, and while she sewed, she sang for her father. The lamp continued to burn steadily at the tower window as she worked. With twice the amount of work to do, she <u>labored</u> long after dusk. She fed the flame more oil and sent her needle skimming through the heavy fabrics. Nimbly her fingers braided shiny cords and coiled them into butterfly buttons. And when the wick sputtered into light each evening, Yenna's heart soared momentarily into her love's memories. Nights passed into weeks, months turned into years, and four years quickly flew by.

13   One day a dusty traveler came into the store and flung a bundle of ragged clothes onto the counter. Yenna shook out the first shirt, and out rolled a ginger root. Taking it into her hand, she saw that pieces had been nibbled off, but the core of the root was still firm and fragrant.

14   She looked up. There stood the man she had promised to wait for. His eyes appeared older and wiser.

15   "Your gift saved my life several times," he said. "The fire of the ginger is powerful indeed."

16   "Why is the ginger root still firm and heavy?" she wondered. "Should it not have dried and withered?"

17   "I kept it close to my heart and my sweat coated it. In lonely moments, my tears soaked it." His calloused[2] hands reached out for her. "Your face has not changed."

18   "Nor has my heart," she replied. "I have kept a lamp burning all these years."

19   "So I have heard," he smiled. "Will you come away with me now? It has taken many years to gather enough gold to buy a farm. I have built you a house on my land."

20   For the first time since his departure, tears cascaded down Yenna's face. She shook her head. "I cannot leave. My father needs me."

---

2. **calloused:** rough; having thickened areas of skin (calluses) caused by repeated rubbing or scraping.

21   "Please come with me," the young man pleaded. "You will be very happy, I promise."

My notes about what I am reading

22   Yenna swept the wetness from her cheeks. "Stay with me and work this store instead," she implored.

23   The young man stiffened and stated proudly, "A man does not live in his wife's house." And the eyes that she remembered so well gleamed with determination.

24   "But this is a new land," she cried. "Must we forever follow the old ways?"

25   She reached out for him, but he brushed her away. With a curse, he hurled the ginger root into the fireplace. As the flames leapt up, Yenna's eyes blurred. The young man clenched and unclenched his fists in anger. They stood like stone.

26   At last the man turned to leave, but suddenly he knelt at the fireplace. Yenna saw him reach in with the tongs and pull something out of the flames.

27   "Look!" he whispered in amazement. "The ginger refuses to be burnt! The flames cannot touch it!"

28   Yenna looked and saw black burn marks charring the root, but when she took it in her hand, she found it still firm and moist. She held it to her nose, and found the fragrant sharpness still there.

29   The couple embraced and swore to stay together. They were married at a lavish banquet attended by all of Chinatown. There, the father passed his fingers over his son-in-law's face and nodded in satisfaction.

30   Shortly after, the merchant Chang died, and the young couple moved away. Yenna sold the business and locked up the tower room. But on nights when boats pull in from far away, they say a flicker of light can still be seen in that high window. And Chinese women are reminded that ginger is one of their best friends.

Use "Ginger for the Heart" (pp. 68–71) to answer questions 1–8.

---

1 What is the purpose of the sensory language in paragraphs 1–3?

A It uses vivid imagery to introduce the main characters.

B It helps readers visualize the story's setting.

C It creates suspense by making the tower room sound dangerous.

D It gives readers clues about the story's main conflict.

2 Which of the following passages from the story shows the author's internal development of a character?

F *His daughter's name was Yenna, and her beauty was beyond compare. She had ivory skin, sparkling eyes, and her hair hung long and silken, shining like polished ebony.*

G *One day, a young man came into the store laden with garments for mending. His shoulders were broad and strong, yet his eyes were soft and caring.*

H *And when the wick sputtered into light each evening, Yenna's heart soared momentarily into her love's memories.*

J *For the first time since his departure, tears cascaded down Yenna's face. She shook her head. "I cannot leave. My father needs me."*

3 What does the ginger in this story most likely represent?

A Enduring love

B The aging process

C Obedience

D Wisdom gained through experience

4 From the details of the story, what can you conclude about traditional Chinese customs?

F Most women did not marry until they were past thirty.

G Young women usually married for love.

H Young men rarely left home to find work.

J Most men thought it shameful to be supported by their wives' families.

5 Which of these elements of mythic or traditional literature is incorporated into the story as a key element of the plot?

A A wise elder

B A hero or heroine with supernatural powers

C A wish granted in an unexpected way

D A magical token or object

6 Examine the context in which <u>labored</u> is used in paragraph 12. Although the word is a synonym for *worked,* what can you conclude about the nuances or connotations of its meaning?

F It suggests working at something boring and unimportant.

G It suggests working hard at something difficult.

H It suggests working in a sloppy way.

J It suggests working together as part of a community or group.

7 Which of these comments on the human condition expresses a main theme of the story?

  A It is honorable to care for one's parents when they are old.

  B People who go against traditional customs often face scorn from their community.

  C True love cannot be extinguished by separation or by social pressure.

  D Modern ways are better than old-fashioned ways.

8 Which of these details would be most important to include in a summary of the story?

  F Yenna has hair like polished ebony.

  G Yenna is a fine seamstress whose buttonholes never stretch out of shape.

  H Yenna gives the man she loves a piece of ginger.

  J Yenna's suitors give her fine gifts.

GO ON

Answer the following question in the space provided.

9 Compare and contrast the characters of Yenna and the man she loves. In what ways are their life experiences and worldviews similar, and in what ways are they different? Explain your answer and support it with evidence from the story.

STOP

Name _____ Date _____

Reading Practice

Read this selection. Then answer the questions that follow.

Leaving Home
by Naomi Shihab Nye

My notes about
what I am reading

*Palestinian American author Naomi Shihab Nye has always
been a traveler. Growing up, she lived in St. Louis, Jerusalem,
and San Antonio. In this essay, she reflects on her nomadic, or
wandering, ways.*

For this traveler, the road ahead also looks back.

1   Our ancestors were nomads, my father tells us. Later
they settled in Jerusalem, but our earlier Arab elders "ran
horses" across Egyptian deserts and the hills of Palestine.
My own grandmother carried her treasures—money, comb,
key—inside her belt. She wore pajamas under her long dress
so she never had to carry them.

2   No wonder I pressed my face to the windows when we
lived near Jerusalem in the mid 1960s, listening to the drums
of gypsies camped in a nearby field. They sounded like
thrumming[1] wheels on a road—one morning soon the field
would empty. I wanted to live with such beautiful, endless
motion.

3   So I grew into an adult who travels almost every week. It's
genetic. When I'm lucky, my husband and son travel with me.
I'm an expert at cleaning the refrigerator before departure—
adios to the solitary whole-wheat heel, the final freezer-
burned waffle. Travel keeps us honest in some essential way.

4   When someone asks where I was born, I want to say
Everywhere. I admit my affection for the mixed scents
of airports—coffee, fresh magazines. I feast my people-
watching gaze, cherishing the airport's anonymity.[2] Who are
you? I'm Gate 42.

5   Maybe this time we're flying to Alaska, which causes our
baggage to look puffier than when we left for Hawaii. Maybe
we're off to Mexico City for a whirlwind weekend of museums

---

1. **thrumming:** making a repetitive, droning sound.
2. **anonymity:** the quality of being unknown or surrounded by strangers.

"Leaving Home" by Naomi Shihab Nye from *Texas Journey,* May/June 1997. Copyright © 1997 by
Naomi Shihab Nye. Reprinted by permission of the author.

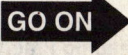
GO ON

and mercados.[3] Maybe it's back up to Oregon, one of our frequent friendly destinations, or off for an intensive New York business day. (With so many choices, how do those New Yorkers choose where to eat? I always let my hosts decide.)

6   Maybe we're just hitting old Highway 90 west from San Antonio toward Big Bend National Park. After travels through Asia, the Middle East, and Latin America, there's no trip more treasured in our minds.

7   For Big Bend, I pack two pairs of blue jeans, a blue-jean vest, and a blue-jean jacket. Navy blue sweatshirt for chilly mornings. Hiking shoes? Long johns? We load the car with water, tangerines, sunflower seeds (my Arab grandmother carried those too)—a little sustenance for 80-mile stretches between West Texas towns. Our son, age 10, collects his "navigation notebook" for copying signs, mileage, and weather details. Blooming yuccas? Tiny shed with cactus growing out of its roof? We never go anywhere without blank paper.

8   Out of San Antonio only 20 minutes, we stop to buy cheese pockets at Haby's Alsatian Bakery in Castroville. One's personal landmarks must never be neglected. Whether it's that festive enchilada restaurant in Del Rio or the Pecos River lookout point, we pull over and pause. Little stops are the charms on the bracelet.

9   Though I resist, with a vengeance, "generic" shopping in cities, it's easy to stop at aging hardware stores in any small town. Try the downtown department store in Sanderson, Texas, for pleasure. Inside, multihued[4] bandannas and shiny pocketknives line the shelves . . . and what do I purchase? A cookie sheet! Three hundred miles from my oven.

10   At Big Bend, we stay in a national park cabin where javelinas poke their noses to the screen at dawn. We drive hundreds of miles on two-lanes and gravel, examining relics of homesteads and dry creek beds. We hike, pause, talk, pause, and rhapsodize[5] against a giant horizon. There's nothing more mind-settling than miles unreeling quietly. Everything seems possible out here in the Kingdom of Quietude.

11   The minute you leave home, your home grows. Now the whole sky is your ceiling. Did you forget anything? No matter. You'll find more than you left behind.

---

3. **mercados:** Spanish for "markets."
4. **multihued:** having many colors.
5. **rhapsodize:** to express oneself in a very enthusiastic way.

GO ON →

Use "Leaving Home" (pp. 75–76) to answer questions 1–7.

1 What is the author's main purpose in writing this essay?

A To express her feelings about her childhood in Jerusalem

B To explain and share her love of travel

C To argue that the love of travel runs in families

D To persuade readers to give up their settled lives and become nomads

2 Note the author's repetition of "Maybe" to begin sentences in paragraphs 5 and 6. What meaning is conveyed by this repetition?

F In any given week, the author and her family might be traveling anywhere in the world.

G The author does not plan her trips in advance, preferring to act on her whims each week.

H The author's family is never sure where she goes when she leaves on a business trip.

J To protect her anonymity, the author is not specific about where she will be traveling next.

3 Paragraph 8 ends with a metaphor: "Little stops are the charms on the bracelet." What idea does this metaphor convey?

A Making local stops along the way adds interest and charm to a trip.

B Small towns along a road often have links to one another.

C Travelers can find bargains when they shop in charming local stores.

D Travelers will find car trips more enjoyable if they stop frequently to stretch their legs.

4 The literal meaning of <u>generic</u> is "general; not specific." What nuance or connotation does the word have in the context of paragraph 9?

F All-inclusive

G Boring

H Expensive

J Repulsive

5 The author repeats the word *pause* in the third sentence of paragraph 10. What meaning does she convey through this repetition?

A The natural world is full of variety.

B The author and her family have trouble communicating with one another.

C It is rare for the author to find peace and tranquility.

D Although the author and her family are active, they also take time to reflect.

GO ON

6 Study the diagram below, which shows a controlling idea of the selection and several details that support it.

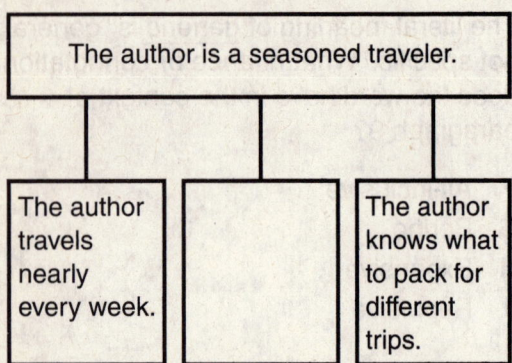

Which of the following details belongs in the empty box?

F The author's grandmother was a seasoned traveler.

G The author has visited Big Bend National Park.

H The author is expert in cleaning out the refrigerator before travel.

J The author enjoys people-watching in airports.

7 Which sentence expresses the essay's central theme with a comment on the human condition?

A *[T]here's no trip more treasured in our minds.*

B *Little stops are the charms on the bracelet.*

C *Everything seems possible out here in the Kingdom of Quietude.*

D *The minute you leave home, your home grows.*

Answer the following question in the space provided.

8 The author ends her essay by encouraging readers to experience the joys of travel. Which parts of the essay, if any, made you feel inclined to follow her advice? Why? Support your answer with evidence from the selection.

Reading Practice

Read this selection. Then answer the questions that follow.

After Apple-Picking

by Robert Frost

My notes about
what I am reading

My long two-pointed ladder's sticking through a tree
Toward heaven still,
And there's a barrel that I didn't fill
Beside it, and there may be two or three
5 Apples I didn't pick upon some bough.
But I am done with apple-picking now.
Essence of winter sleep is on the night,
The scent of apples: I am drowsing off.
I cannot rub the strangeness from my sight
10 I got from looking through a pane of glass
I skimmed this morning from the drinking trough
And held against the world of <u>hoary</u> grass.
It melted, and I let it fall and break.
But I was well
15 Upon my way to sleep before it fell,
And I could tell
What form my dreaming was about to take.
Magnified apples appear and disappear,
Stem end and blossom end,
20 And every fleck of russet showing clear.
My instep arch not only keeps the ache,
It keeps the pressure of a ladder-round.
I feel the ladder sway as the boughs bend.
And I keep hearing from the cellar bin
25 The rumbling sound
Of load on load of apples coming in.
For I have had too much
Of apple-picking: I am overtired

GO ON

Of the great harvest I myself desired.
30 There were ten thousand thousand fruit to touch,
Cherish in hand, lift down, and not let fall.
For all
That struck the earth,
No matter if not bruised or spiked with stubble,
35 Went surely to the cider-apple heap
As of no worth.
One can see what will trouble
This sleep of mine, whatever sleep it is.
Were he not gone,
40 The woodchuck could say whether it's like his
Long sleep, as I describe its coming on,
Or just some human sleep.

My notes about
what I am reading

Use "After Apple-Picking" (pp. 80–81) to answer questions 1–5.

---

1 What is the rhyme scheme of lines 1–6 of the poem?

A *abbacc*

B *ababcd*

C *aabbcc*

D *ababab*

2 The phrase "Toward heaven still" in line 2 can best be described as —

F a literal description

G an extended metaphor

H an iambic foot

J a biblical or mythological allusion

3 Read these lines from the poem.

> *I cannot rub the strangeness from my sight*
> *I got from looking through a pane of glass*
> *I skimmed this morning from the drinking trough*
> *And held against the world of <u>hoary</u> grass.*

The word <u>hoary</u> means "turned gray or white with old age." Why does the speaker use this word to describe the grass?

A The speaker is dreaming and thinks the lawn is the beard of an old man.

B The grass looks silvery because it is covered with morning frost.

C The lawn has died, turning from green to a grayish brown.

D The speaker realizes that the grass is ready for haying.

4 Sensory images make the speaker's experience vivid. To which senses does the poem appeal in lines 18–26?

F Hearing, taste, sight

G Taste, hearing, smell

H Touch, smell

J Sight, touch, hearing

5 The speaker of the poem is —

A pleased at the results of his hard work

B disappointed that his hard work did not pay off with a larger harvest

C weary from achieving the goal he once desired

D worried because so much of his harvest was damaged

GO ON

Name _____ Date _____

Answer the following question in the space provided.

6 The word *sleep* is repeated several times in the poem. What meaning might this have for the speaker, and what broader theme about life is suggested by the speaker's reflections on sleep? Provide examples from the poem to support your answer.

Name _____ Date _____

Reading Practice

Read this selection. Then answer the questions that follow.

from In the Fog

by Milton Geiger

My notes about
what I am reading

*On a foggy night, a man steps out of his car to read a street sign.
He is approached by two bearded men who point a gun at him but
tell him not to be afraid. When they learn he is a doctor, they lead
him to another man who is badly injured.*

[*A wounded man is lying against a section of stone fence.
He, too, is bearded, though very young, and his shirt is dark
with blood. He breathes but never stirs otherwise.* Eben
enters, followed by the Doctor *and* Zeke.]

5   **Zeke.** Ain't stirred a mite since we left 'im.

Doctor. Let's have that lantern here! (*The* Doctor *tears the
man's shirt for better access to the wound. Softly*) Dreadful!
Dreadful . . . !

Zeke's voice (*off scene*). Reckon it's bad in the chest like
10   that, hey?

Doctor (*taking pulse*). His pulse is positively racing . . . ! How
long has he been this way?

Zeke. A long time, mister. A long time. . . .

Doctor (*to* Eben). You! Hand me my bag.

15   [Eben *puts down lantern and hands bag to* Doctor. *The*
Doctor *opens bag and takes out a couple of retractors.*[1] Zeke
holds lantern close now.]

Doctor. Lend me a hand with these retractors. (*He works on
the man.*) All right . . . when I tell you to draw back on the
20   retractors—draw back.

Eben. Aye.

Zeke. How is 'e, mister?

---

1. **retractors:** surgical instruments for holding back the flesh at the edge of a wound.

GO ON ➡

My notes about
what I am reading

Doctor (*preoccupied*). More retraction. Pull them a bit more. Hold it. . . .

25   **Eben.** Bad, ain't he?

Doctor. Bad enough. The bullet didn't touch any lung tissue far as I can see right now. There's some pneumothorax[2] though. All I can do now is plug the wound. There's some cotton and gauze wadding in my bag. Find it. . . .

30   [Zeke *probes about silently in the bag and comes up with a small dark box of gauze.*]

Doctor. That's it. (*Works a moment in silence*) I've never seen anything quite like it.

Eben. Yer young, doctor. Lot's o' things you've never seen.

35   **Doctor.** Adhesive tape!

[Zeke *finds a roll of three-inch tape and hands it to the* Doctor, *who tears off long strips and slaps them on the dressing and pats and smooths them to man's chest.* Eben *replaces equipment in* Doctor's *bag and closes it with a hint*

40   *of the finality to come. A preview of dismissal, so to speak.*]

Doctor (*at length*). There. So much for that. Now then— (*Takes man's shoulders*) give me a hand here.

Zeke (*quiet suspicion*). What fer?

Doctor. We've got to move this man.

45   **Zeke.** What fer?

Doctor (*stands; indignantly*). We've got to get him to a hospital for treatment; a thorough cleansing of the wound; irrigation.[3] I've done all I can for him here.

Zeke. I reckon he'll be all right 'thout no hospital.

50   **Doctor.** Do you realize how badly this man's hurt!

Eben. He won't bleed to death, will he?

Doctor. I don't think so—not with that plug and pressure dressing. But bleeding isn't the only danger we've got to—

Zeke (*interrupts*). All right, then. Much obliged to you.

55   **Doctor.** This man's dangerously hurt!

2. **pneumothorax:** air or gas in the chest cavity.
3. **irrigation:** here, flushing out a wound with water or other fluid.

Zeke. Reckon he'll pull through now, thanks to you.

Doctor. I'm glad you feel that way about it! But I'm going to report this to the Pennsylvania State Police at the first telephone I reach!

60 **Zeke.** We ain't stoppin' ye, mister.

Eben. Fog is liftin', Zeke. Better be done with this, I say.

Zeke (*nods, sadly*). Aye. Ye can go now, mister . . . and thanks. (*Continues*) We never meant a mite o' harm, I can tell ye. If we killed, it was no wish of ours.

65 **Eben.** What's done is done. Aye.

Zeke. Ye can go now, stranger. . . .

[Eben *hands* Zeke *the* Doctor*'s bag.* Zeke *hands it gently to the* Doctor.]

Doctor. Very well. You haven't heard the last of this, though!

70 **Zeke.** That's the truth, mister. We've killed, aye; and we've been hurt for it. . . .

Eben. Hurt bad.

[*The* Doctor*'s face is puckered with doubt and strange apprehension.*]

75 **Zeke.** We're not alone, mister. We ain't the only ones. (*Sighs*)
Ye
can go now, doctor . . . and our thanks to ye. . . .

[*The* Doctor *leaves the other two, still gazing at them in strange enchantment and wonder and a touch of indignation.*]

80 **Eben's voice.** Thanks mister. . . .

Zeke's voice. In the name o' mercy . . . We thank you. . . .

Eben. In the name o' mercy.

Zeke. Thanks, mister. . . .

Eben. In the name o' kindness. . . .

85 [*The two men stand with their wounded comrade at their feet—like a group statue in the park. The fog thickens across*

GO ON ➡

*the scene. Far off the long, sad wail of a locomotive
whimpers in the dark.*

My notes about
what I am reading

90 *The scene now shifts to a young* Attendant *standing in
front of a gasoline pump taking a reading and recording it in
a book as he prepares to close up. He turns as he hears the
car approach on the gravel drive.*

The Doctor *enters.*]

Attendant (*pleasantly*). Good evening, sir. (*Nods off at car*)
95 Care to pull 'er up to this pump, sir? Closing up.

Doctor (*impatiently*). No. Where's your telephone, please?
I've just been held up!

Attendant. Pay station inside, sir. . . .

Doctor. Thank you! (*The* Doctor *starts to go past the*
100 Attendant.)

Attendant. Excuse me, sir. . . .

Doctor (*stops*). Eh, what is it, what is it?

Attendant. Uh . . . what sort of looking fellows were they?

Doctor. Oh—two big fellows with a rifle; faces and heads
105 bandaged and smeared with dirt and blood. Friend of theirs
with a gaping hole in his chest. I'm a doctor, so they forced
me to <u>attend</u> him. Why?

Attendant. *Those* fellers, huh?

Doctor. Then you know about them!

110 **Attendant.** I guess so.

Doctor. They're armed and they're desperate!

Attendant. That was about two or three miles back, would
you say?

Doctor (*fumbling in pocket*). Just about—I don't seem to
115 have the change. I wonder if you'd spare me change for a
quarter . . . ?

Attendant (*makes change from metal coin canister at his
belt*). Certainly, sir. . . .

Doctor. What town was that back there, now?

My notes about
what I am reading

120 **Attendant** (*dumps coins in other's hand*). There you are, sir.

Doctor (*impatient*). Yes, thank you. I say—what town was that back there, so I can tell the police?

Attendant. That was . . . Gettysburg, mister. . . .

Doctor. Gettysburg . . . ?

125 **Attendant.** Gettysburg and Gettysburg battlefield. . . . (*Looks off*) When it's light and the fog's gone, you can see the gravestones. Meade's men . . . Pickett's men, Robert E. Lee's.[4] . . .

[*The* Doctor *is looking off with the* Attendant; *now he turns
130 his head slowly to stare at the other man.*]

Attendant (*continues*). On nights like this—well—you're not the first those men've stopped . . . or the last. (*Nods off*) Fill 'er up, mister?

Doctor. Yes, fill 'er up. . . .

---

4. **Meade's men . . . Lee's:** The Battle of Gettysburg was a turning point in the Civil War. On July 1–3, 1863, the Confederacy's forces, under Robert E. Lee, met the Union forces, under George Gordon Meade. The climax of the battle came when 15,000 Confederate soldiers, led by George Pickett, charged Cemetery Ridge and were repelled. The North suffered about 23,000 casualties; the South about 20,000.

GO ON ➡

Use the excerpt from "In the Fog" (pp. 84–88) to answer questions 1–8.

1 "In the Fog" is a —

A tragedy

B mystery

C comedy

D farce

2 One clue that the play involves characters from another time in history is —

F the men's old-fashioned dialect

G the doctor's equipment

H the fog

J the stone fence

3 Why do Zeke and Eben stop people who are passing through the fog?

A To get help for the wounded man

B To describe the Battle of Gettysburg

C To take the wounded man to a hospital

D To protect travelers from harm

4 Zeke and Eben are the ghosts of —

F murderers

G hunters

H motorists

J soldiers

5 In line 64, Zeke says, "If we killed, it was no wish of ours." He is referring to —

A their friend's likely death after Zeke shot him accidentally

B the fact that in war soldiers must follow all orders, even to kill

C their gratitude that the wounded man has survived

D how they have hurt other people driving through the fog

6 The stage directions in lines 85–88 compare the men to a "group statue in the park." This image is meant to remind the audience of a —

F family portrait

G scene from a play

H group of students

J war monument

7 Read the following dictionary entry.

> **attend** \ə tĕnd´\ *v.* **1.** to be present at **2.** to take care of **3.** to listen to **4.** to take charge of

What is the definition of <u>attend</u> as it is used in line 105 of the play?

A Definition 1

B Definition 2

C Definition 3

D Definition 4

8 The main conflict of the play occurs when —

F the doctor struggles to treat the wounded man

G the men will not allow the doctor to take the wounded man to the hospital

H the doctor tries to call the police from the gas station

J the attendant tells the doctor who the men in the fog are

Name _____ Date _____

9 How does the author create suspense in the play? Give three examples.

STOP

Reading Practice

Read this selection. Then answer the questions that follow.

9/11 Dogs Seemed to Escape Illnesses

by Amy Westfeldt

My notes about
what I am reading

*On September 11, 2001, four planes were hijacked by terrorists
and used to attack targets in the United States. Two of the planes
crashed into the twin towers of the World Trade Center in New York
City. After the towers collapsed, the site became known as "ground
zero." The effort to rescue survivors and find the bodies of the dead
involved both human and canine workers.*

1   NEW YORK — They dug in the toxic World Trade Center
dust for survivors, and later for the dead. Their feet were
burned by white-hot <u>debris</u>. But unlike thousands of others
who toiled at ground zero after Sept. 11, these rescue
workers aren't sick.

2   Scientists have spent years studying the health of search-
and-rescue dogs that nosed through the debris at ground
zero, and to their surprise, they have found no sign of major
illness in the animals.

3   They are trying to figure out why this is so.

4   "They didn't have any airway protection, they didn't have
any skin protection. They were sort of in the worst of it," said
Cynthia Otto, a veterinarian at the University of Pennsylvania,
where researchers launched a study of 97 dogs five years
ago.

5   Although many ground zero dogs have died—some of
rare cancers—researchers say many have lived beyond the
average life span for dogs and are not getting any sicker than
average.

6   Owners of the dogs dispute the findings, saying there is a
definite link between the toxic air and their pets' health.

GO ON ➡

7   Otto has tracked dogs that spent an average of 10 days after the 2001 terrorist attacks at either the trade center site, the landfill in New York where most of the debris was taken, or the heavily damaged Pentagon.

8   As of last month, she said, 30 percent of the dogs deployed after Sept. 11 had died, compared with 22 percent of those in a comparison group of dogs who were not pressed into service. The difference was not considered statistically significant,[1] Otto said.

9   But she added: "We have to keep looking."

10   A separate study, to be published soon by a doctor at New York's Animal Medical Center, focused on about two dozen New York police dogs and comes to similar conclusions.

11   The results have baffled doctors. A study released last month found that 70 percent of the people who worked at ground zero suffer severe respiratory[2] problems; scientists thought that the dogs might have similar health problems.

12   The dogs' owners and scientists have many theories why dogs aren't showing the same level of illness as people. Their noses are longer, possibly serving as a filter to protect their lungs from toxic dust and other debris, they say. The dogs were at the site an average of several days, while many people who report lung disease and cancer spent months cleaning up after the attacks.

13   The research isn't persuasive to many owners of dogs that died after working at the trade center site.

14   Joaquin Guerrero, a police officer in Saginaw, Mich., took two dogs, Felony and Rookie, to ground zero for 10 days after the attacks. While Felony remains healthy, Rookie died at age 9 in 2004 of cancer of the mouth. Guerrero believes his death was caused by exposure to ground zero.

1. **statistically significant:** unlikely to occur by chance. In the case of the 30 percent of rescue dogs who died, Otto means that this percentage is not sufficiently larger than the 22 percent of other dogs who died to attribute the higher rate of death to the rescue dogs' work at ground zero.
2. **respiratory:** related to breathing.

GO ON

15   "If the people are getting it, you know dogs are showing signs of it," Guerrero said.

16   Scott Shields' golden retriever, Bear, located the body of a fire chief and many other victims at ground zero. The 11-year-old dog died a year after the attacks of several types of cancer.

17   "He had never been sick a day in his life" before going to the site, where he sustained a wound to his back from steel debris, Shields said.

18   Shields, who heads a search-and-rescue dog foundation named after Bear, said Bear "died from bad government" and the toxic air at ground zero. He said that studies under way should have included every dog that worked at the site, and that the Penn study is flawed because it tries to compare dogs that worked at the Pentagon as well as New York.

19   Otto said that some of the dogs that worked at the sites could not be found and other dogs' owners were not willing to subject their pets to annual blood tests and X-rays.

20   Mary Flood, whose 11 ½-year-old black Labrador, Jake, is completely healthy five years after working at ground zero, said that dogs' much shorter life span may also make it harder to track long-term illness.

21   "Maybe there's not enough time to develop these things before they're no longer with us," she said.

Use "9/11 Dogs Seemed to Escape Illnesses" (pp. 91–93) to answer questions 1–6.

1 As it is used in paragraphs 1 and 2, the word <u>debris</u> means —

A a substance that is very hot

B litter spread over a large area

C a landfill like the one in New York City

D the remains of something destroyed

2 Scientists who study dogs that worked at ground zero believe that —

F dogs that worked at ground zero longer than other dogs did not get any sicker

G most of the dogs that worked at ground zero did not become sick

H many dogs developed respiratory illnesses and cancer

J the dogs' longer noses make them more likely to develop illness than humans

3 The author's purpose in presenting the information in the article is to —

A persuade readers to accept the owners' arguments about individual dogs

B suggest that more dogs need to be included in the study for validity's sake

C claim that sufficient research has been done about the subject

D give a balanced view of the debate between scientists and dog owners

4 Which of the following statements from the article expresses an opinion?

F *The results have baffled doctors.*

G *They didn't have any airway protection, they didn't have any skin protection....*

H *As of last month ... 30 percent of the dogs deployed after Sept. 11 had died....*

J *[S]tudies ... should have included every dog that worked at the site....*

5 This article's tone is best described as —

A objective, because the author wants to to share information on both sides of the issue and let readers draw their own conclusions

B sarcastic, because the author wants to belittle the view that 9/11 rescue dogs have not suffered serious health consequences

C amused, because the author believes there is no way to know the effect on rescue dogs and wants to poke fun at people who argue about it

D angry, because the author believes not enough is being done to study the effects on rescue dogs and wants readers to share her outrage

6 Which of the following is the best summary of the article?

F Scientists expected rescue dogs who worked at ground zero to suffer the same health consequences, such as respiratory problems, as human rescue workers. However, several studies have proven that this is not the case.

G Several scientific studies indicate that rescue dogs who worked at ground zero have not suffered greater rates of illness than dogs who did not. However, some people whose dogs have died after working at the site dispute the findings.

H Rescue dogs who worked at ground zero, such as a golden retriever named Bear, died of cancer soon afterward. It's clear that the two events are related, and more studies must be done.

J Scientists who study the effects of working at ground zero on rescue dogs do not always agree with the owners of dogs who died after doing the work. Both groups care about the issue and have drawn conclusions from what they have observed.

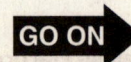

Answer the following question in the space provided.

7 The writer presents evidence from each group—scientists and dog owners—about the health of the dogs over time. Whose conclusions do you find most convincing, and why? Support your answer with evidence from the selection.

STOP

Reading Practice

Read this selection. Then answer the questions that follow.

Good Parents Don't Allow Teens to Circumnavigate

by Leonard Pitts

My notes about
what I am reading

In 2010, 16-year-old Abby Sunderland tried to become the youngest person to sail around the world without assistance. The trip was highly controversial. Many people, such as the author of this editorial, questioned why her parents would allow her to make such a difficult and dangerous journey by herself. Abby and her family argued that she was a well-prepared and experienced sailor.

1   And now, a rebuttal from inside the cotton-wool tunnel.

2   That, according to Laurence Sunderland, is the safe, heavily padded place where critics of him, his wife Marianne, and their 16-year-old daughter Abby live, cushioned from life's dangers and risks. If the names sound familiar, there's a reason. Abby Sunderland is the California girl whose attempt to become the youngest person to ever circumnavigate the globe ended in near tragedy when her boat became crippled by storms in the Indian Ocean. Laurence and Marianne are the parents who let her go.

3   The girl was found and rescued last week, but her brush with disaster has earned her folks international reproach. A writer on a Los Angeles Times message board called them "moron parents." A reader of The Herald Sun in Australia accused them of "child abuse and neglect."

4   But the Sunderlands are unrepentant. The issue, says Laurence Sunderland, a boat builder, is not his daughter's age, but her competence; she has been sailing all her life. He sees his family—including teenage son Zac, who sailed the globe last year, as adventurers. "Sailing and life in general

---

"Taking the ultimate risk—all in the name of TV fame" (Retitled: "Good Parents Don't Allow Teens to Circumnavigate") by Leonard Pitts from *The Miami Herald,* June 16, 2010. Copyright © 2010 by The Miami Herald. Reprinted by permission of the Miami Herald Media Company.

GO ON ➡

My notes about
what I am reading

is dangerous," he told The Associated Press. "Teenagers drive cars. Does that mean teenagers shouldn't drive a car? I think people who hold that opinion have lost their zeal for life. They're living in a cotton-wool tunnel to make everything safe."

5   But the hole in Sunderland's logic is wide enough to sail a crippled boat through. Yes, driving is dangerous—though probably not as dangerous as sailing alone around the world. If you don't take that relatively small risk, though, your ability to get from Point A to Point B and indeed, your very independence, are significantly compromised. There is a compelling reason to drive.

6   There was NO compelling reason for Abby's voyage. She was hardly Ferdinand Magellan seeking a western route to the Spice Islands. Rather, she was a teenager from Thousand Oaks, Calif., whose parents allowed her to risk her life in search of a dubious, and ultimately meaningless, record.

7   The effort to rescue her involved the Australian Maritime Safety Authority, a search plane and a French fishing boat. According to Australian newspapers, this will cost taxpayers there hundreds of thousands of dollars. Not to mention the risk for the sailors who saved Abby; the French captain fell into the ocean and had to be rescued himself.

8   All that, and for what?

9   Well, it will surprise no one to hear the Sunderlands were shopping a reality show. Laurence claims he pulled out of "Adventures in Sunderland" before Abby sailed, when it became clear he and the producers had dissimilar visions. He wanted an inspirational program celebrating a family of daredevils and risk-takers; they wanted to chronicle what they saw as a family sending a daughter off to certain death.

10   Cynical as they might have been, his erstwhile partners evidently had a clearer view of things than Sunderland did.

11   There are obvious echoes here. Echoes of the Heene family whose balloon boy hoax[1] last year was tied to a TV reality show proposal. And of Jessica Dubroff, who died in a crash at age 7 while attempting, before TV news cameras, to become the youngest pilot ever to fly across the country.

12   The common thread? Parents narcissistic enough to believe they belonged on television and calculating enough to exploit their own children to get there. Perhaps that is only to be expected in an era where fame has become downsized and cheapened until it is a thing seemingly anyone can have if they are, or do something, outlandish enough.

13   Laurence Sunderland surely qualifies. He sent his daughter to sea all alone for no good reason. But for the grace of God, she would be dead now.

14   And the view from inside the cotton-wool tunnel is looking better all the time.

1. **balloon boy hoax:** On October 15, 2009, a hot-air balloon floated above eastern Colorado, and the parents of a six-year-old boy told the media that their son might be inside it. The boy was not in the balloon and later confessed that the event had been a publicity stunt.

GO ON ➡

Use "Good Parents Don't Allow Teens to Circumnavigate" (pp. 96–98) to answer questions 1–7.

1 Which of the following best expresses the editorial's main purpose?

A To argue that Abby Sunderland's parents were foolish and selfish to allow her to sail around the world alone

B To persuade people to discourage teenagers from operating sailboats in the ocean

C To discuss reality shows that encourage people to take risks

D To explain the role of the Australian Maritime Safety Authority

2 Which of the following best expresses Abby's parents' argument in support of her journey?

F They could not stop her.

G Teenagers should learn to sail.

H Her trip was not going to be dangerous.

J People should not be afraid to take risks.

3 Laurence Sunderland argued that "sailing and life in general is dangerous. . . . Teenagers drive cars. Does that mean teenagers shouldn't drive a car?" Which of the following summarizes the writer's counterargument to this idea?

A There are many driver education courses available to teach teenagers how to drive.

B Teenagers shouldn't drive cars or operate sailboats alone.

C Driving a car is a necessary risk, while sailing around the world alone is not.

D Abby did not have enough experience to operate a sailboat.

4 Read this sentence from paragraph 12.

Perhaps that is only to be expected in an era where fame has become downsized and cheapened until it is a thing seemingly anyone can have if they are, or do something, outlandish enough.

What conclusion does the writer make through deductive reasoning, based on the principle above?

F The money spent to rescue Abby came out of taxpayers' pockets.

G Jessica Dubroff should not have taken flying lessons.

H People who avoid risk shouldn't preach to those who embrace it.

J Abby's parents willingly exploited their child for fame.

5 The word narcissistic means "vain" or "self-admiring." In the context of paragraph 12, what nuance of meaning does the word suggest?

A These parents believe they are extremely good-looking.

B These parents believe their lives are so interesting that everyone else would want to know about them.

C These parents believe they are smart enough to be successful TV executives.

D These parents don't care for their children and are only interested in pursuing their own dreams.

6 Read these sentences from paragraph 13.

> He sent his daughter to sea all alone for no good reason. But for the grace of God, she would be dead now.

People who disagree with the writer might say that, in these lines, he uses the fallacy known as —

F false analogy

G unqualified generalization

H circular reasoning

J non sequitur

7 Which of the following facts supports the writer's belief that the family put themselves and others at risk?

A Sailors had to rescue Abby, and one of the sailors fell and had to be rescued.

B The parents were hoping to star in a reality show about a family of daredevils.

C Abby's journey ended when she encountered storms in the Indian Ocean.

D The Sunderlands considered themselves a family of adventurers who took risks sailing.

Answer the following question in the space provided.

---

8 Do you agree with the writer of the editorial that Abby's family was wrong and that "good parents don't allow teens to circumnavigate"? Or do you disagree with this statement and feel the writer is unfair to the parents of Abby Sunderland? Support your answer with evidence from the selection.

STOP

Reading Practice

> **Read the next two selections. Then answer the questions that follow.**

from **Appearances Are Destructive**

by Mark Mathabane

*When Mark Mathabane enrolled his sisters in an American public
school, he had high hopes for their success. In South Africa, where
they had been living, a policy of segregation known as apartheid
meant that they had to attend black schools, which were inferior in
every way to the white schools. By contrast, he viewed American
schools as "Shangri-Las," or paradises. However, the lack of a dress
code resulted in problems for his sisters.*

1   As public schools reopen for the new year, strategies
to curb school violence will once again be hotly debated.
Installing metal detectors and hiring security guards will help,
but the experience of my two sisters makes a compelling
case for greater use of dress codes as a way to protect
students and promote learning.

2   Shortly after my sisters arrived here from South Africa
I enrolled them at the local public school. I had great
expectations for their educational experience. Compared
with black schools under apartheid, American schools
are Shangri-Las, with modern textbooks, school buses,
computers, libraries, lunch programs and dedicated teachers.

3   But despite these benefits, which students in many parts
of the world only dream about, my sisters' efforts at learning
were almost derailed. They were constantly taunted for their
homely outfits. A couple of times they came home in tears. In
South Africa students were required to wear uniforms, so my
sisters had never been preoccupied with clothes and jewelry.

4   They became so distraught that they insisted on
transferring to different schools, despite my reassurances
that there was nothing wrong with them because of what they
wore.

5   I have visited enough public schools around the country
to know that my sisters' experiences are not unique. In
schools in many areas, brand names are more familiar
names to students than Zora Neale Hurston, Shakespeare

Excerpt from "Appearances Are Destructive" by Mark Mathabane from *The New York Times*,
August 26, 1993. Copyright © 1993 by Mark Mathabane. Reprinted by permission of the author.

GO ON ➤

My notes about
what I am reading

and Faulkner. Many students seem to pay more attention to what's on their bodies than in their minds.

6   Teachers have shared their frustrations with me at being unable to teach those students willing to learn because classes are frequently disrupted by other students ogling themselves in mirrors, painting their fingernails, combing their hair, shining their gigantic shoes, or comparing designer labels on jackets, caps and jewelry.

7   The fiercest competition among students is often not over academic achievements, but over who dresses most expensively. And many students now measure parental love by how willing their mothers and fathers are to pamper them with money for the latest fads in clothes, sneakers and jewelry.

8   Those parents without the money to waste on such meretricious[1] extravagances are considered uncaring and cruel. They often watch in dismay and helplessness as their children become involved with gangs and peddle drugs to raise the money.

9   When students are asked why they attach so much importance to clothing, they frequently reply that it's the cool thing to do, that it gives them status and earns them respect. And clothes are also used to send other messages, with girls thinking that the only things that make them attractive to boys are skimpy dresses and gaudy looks, rather than intelligence and academic excellence.

10   The argument by civil libertarians that dress codes infringe on freedom of expression is misleading. We observe dress codes in nearly every aspect of our lives without any diminution[2] of our freedoms—as demonstrated by flight attendants, bus drivers, postal employees, high school bands, military personnel, sports teams, Girl and Boy Scouts, employees of fast-food chains, restaurants and hotels.

11   In many countries where students outperform their American counterparts academically, school dress codes are observed as part of creating the proper learning environment. Their students tend to be neater, less disruptive in class and more disciplined, mainly because their minds are focused more on learning and less on materialism.

12   It's time Americans realized that the benefits of safe and effective schools far outweigh any perceived curtailment[3] of freedom of expression brought on by dress codes.

1. **meretricious:** showy, vulgar.
2. **diminution:** reduction.
3. **curtailment:** lessening.

GO ON ➡

Name _____ Date _____

from Manual on School Uniforms

This selection is from a manual published by the U.S. Department of Education.

Users' Guide to Adopting a School Uniform Policy

The decision whether to adopt a uniform policy is made by states, local school districts, and schools. For uniforms to be a success, as with all other school initiatives, parents must be involved. The following information is provided to assist parents, teachers, and school leaders in determining whether to adopt a school uniform policy.

1. Get parents involved from the beginning

Parental support of a uniform policy is critical for success. Indeed, the strongest push for school uniforms in recent years has come from parent groups who want better discipline in their children's schools. Parent groups have actively lobbied schools to create uniform policies and have often led school task forces that have drawn up uniform guidelines. Many schools that have successfully created a uniform policy survey parents first to gauge support for school uniform requirements and then seek parental input in designing the uniform. Parent support is also essential in encouraging students to wear the uniform.

2. Protect students' religious expression

A school uniform policy must accommodate students whose religious beliefs are substantially burdened by a uniform requirement. As U.S. Secretary of Education Richard W. Riley stated in **Religious Expression in Public Schools,** a guide he sent to superintendents throughout the nation on August 10, 1995:

> Students may display religious messages on items of clothing to the same extent that they are permitted to display other comparable messages. Religious messages may not be singled out for suppression, but rather are subject to the same rules as generally apply to comparable messages. When wearing particular attire, such as yarmulkes[1] and head scarves, during the

---

1. **yarmulkes:** skullcaps worn by some Jewish males.

Excerpt from "Manual on School Uniforms" prepared by the U.S. Department of Education.
Full text available: http://www2.ed.gov/updates/uniforms.html.

GO ON

school day is part of students' religious practice, under the Religious Freedom Restoration Act schools generally may not prohibit the wearing of such items.

My notes about
what I am reading

3. Protect students' other rights of expression

A uniform policy may not prohibit students from wearing or displaying expressive items—for example, a button that supports a political candidate—so long as such items do not independently contribute to disruption by substantially interfering with discipline or with the rights of others. Thus, for example, a uniform policy may prohibit students from wearing a button bearing a gang insignia. A uniform policy may also prohibit items that undermine the integrity of the uniform, notwithstanding their expressive nature, such as a sweatshirt that bears a political message but also covers or replaces the type of shirt required by the uniform policy.

4. Determine whether to have a voluntary or mandatory school uniform policy

Some schools have adopted wholly voluntary school uniform policies which permit students freely to choose whether and under what circumstances they will wear the school uniform. Alternatively, some schools have determined that it is both warranted and more effective to adopt a mandatory uniform policy.

5. When a mandatory school uniform policy is adopted, determine whether to have an "opt out" provision

In most cases, school districts with mandatory policies allow students, normally with parental consent, to "opt out" of the school uniform requirements. . . .

6. Do not require students to wear a message

Schools should not impose a form of expression on students by requiring them to wear uniforms bearing a substantive message, such as a political message.

7. Assist families that need financial help

In many cases, school uniforms are less expensive than the clothing that students typically wear to school. Nonetheless, the cost of purchasing a uniform may be a burden on some families. School districts with uniform policies should make provisions for students whose families are unable to afford uniforms. Many have done so. Examples of the types of

GO ON ➡

assistance include: (a) the school district provides uniforms to students who cannot afford to purchase them; (b) community and business leaders provide uniforms or contribute financial support for uniforms; (c) school parents work together to make uniforms available for economically disadvantaged students; and (d) used uniforms from graduates are made available to incoming students.

My notes about what I am reading

8. Treat school uniforms as part of an overall safety program

Uniforms by themselves cannot solve all of the problems of school discipline, but they can be one positive contributing factor to discipline and safety. Other initiatives that many schools have used in conjunction with uniforms to address specific problems in their community include aggressive truancy reduction initiatives, drug prevention efforts, student-athlete drug testing, community efforts to limit gangs, a zero tolerance policy for weapons, character education classes, and conflict resolution programs. Working with parents, teachers, students, and principals can make a uniform policy part of a strong overall safety program, one that is broadly supported in the community.

Use the excerpt from "Appearances Are Destructive" (pp. 102–103) to answer questions 1–7.

1 What is the author's purpose in this selection?

A To evaluate the quality of education in American schools as compared to those in other countries

B To promote the use of dress codes as a way to make schools more conducive to learning

C To show the extent of prejudice that exists in American public schools

D To urge schools to get metal detectors, security guards, and whatever other measures they need to prevent violence

2 To develop and support his claim, the author relies mostly on —

F statistical research

G anecdotal evidence

H factual analysis

J historical precedents

3 Which words from paragraph 6 best help readers understand the meaning of the word ogling?

A *themselves in mirrors*

B *comparing designer labels*

C *disrupted by other students*

D *those students willing to learn*

4 In paragraphs 1–4, the author's tone is mainly one of —

F anger

G bitterness

H relief

J frustration

5 Which is the best summary of the author's counterargument in paragraph 10?

A Dress codes take away students' freedom of expression.

B Many professions and activities impose dress codes without affecting individual freedoms.

C Parents should stop buying their children so many clothes.

D Civil libertarians are wrong.

6 Which of the following conclusions about uniforms would be a hasty generalization?

F If schools had dress codes, their problems would be solved.

G Asking students to wear uniforms is like asking sunbathers to wear sunscreen.

H School uniforms reduce school violence because schools with uniforms are safer.

J In many American public schools, clothing is seen as a sign of status.

7 Paragraph 12 suggests that Mathabane's intended audience is —

A the public

B high school students

C teachers and administrators

D his sisters

GO ON

Use the excerpt from "Manual on School Uniforms" (pp. 104–106) to answer questions 8–11.

8 What does this document identify as the key factor in implementing a uniform policy?

   F Wealth of the school district

   G Parental approval

   H Administrative control

   J Diversity of the population

9 The specific policies described in guideline 7 are taken from the general principle that —

   A school uniforms cost less than a typical student wardrobe

   B parents have an obligation to help each other

   C not all students should have to wear uniforms

   D families should not face economic hardship to comply with public school rules

10 Which statement identifies the main idea of guideline 8?

   F Districts should adopt measures that have proven to be successful in other schools.

   G Uniforms and zero tolerance policies for weapons and drugs will make schools safer.

   H Uniforms should be one element of a multi-faceted safety and discipline program.

   J Other safety measures, such as conflict resolution programs, will more significantly reduce violence than dress codes.

11 From the tone and diction of this document, it is clear that its purpose is to —

   A persuasively argue the need to implement uniform codes

   B officially inform schools of mandatory dress codes

   C objectively present considerations for shaping policy

   D critically evaluate past efforts to impose dress codes

GO ON

Use the excerpts from "Appearances Are Destructive" and "Manual on School Uniforms" (pp. 102–106) to answer questions 12–14.

---

12 Both selections view uniforms as —

 F an infringement of students' creative expression

 G a difficult policy to enforce without parental support

 H the only solution to increasingly violent schools

 J a way to minimize disruption in the classroom

13 With which provision of "Manual on School Uniforms" would Mathabane most likely agree?

 A A uniform policy should prohibit students from wearing a button bearing a gang insignia.

 B Schools should allow students to "opt out" of the uniform requirements.

 C Schools may choose to adopt wholly voluntary uniform policies that permit students to choose whether or not they wear uniforms.

 D A uniform policy may not prohibit students from wearing or displaying expressive items.

14 Compared to Mathabane, the writers of "Manual on School Uniforms" are more concerned with —

 F levels of academic achievement in schools without uniforms

 G parents' irresponsibility in giving in to their children's demands

 H students' rights

 J peer pressure

GO ON ▶

Name _____ Date _____

15 What do readers learn from reading both selections that they might not understand from reading only one? Explain your answer and support it with evidence from **both** selections.

Written Composition

Name _____ Date _____

Written Composition: Persuasive Essay 1

READ

Read the quotation in the box below.

> "A different language is a different vision of life."
>
> *Federico Fellini*

THINK

Should high school students be required to study a foreign language for two years in order to graduate? Consider the pros and cons of this requirement before deciding how you feel about the issue.

WRITE

Write an essay to be presented to the state board of education in which you express your view about requiring a foreign language for graduation. Support your position with specific reasons and evidence.

As you write your composition, remember to —

☐ craft a thesis that states whether there should be a foreign-language requirement for graduation

☐ organize your argument logically and effectively, using transitions to show relationships between ideas

☐ develop your argument with strong reasons supported by relevant facts and other evidence, and use rhetorical devices to strengthen your argument

☐ make sure your composition is no longer than one page

TEKS 13A, 13B, 13C, 13D, 16A, 16B, 16C, 16F, 17, 18, 19

ANALYZE THE PROMPT
The prompt asks you to write an essay expressing your position on a foreign-language requirement for high school students. You must state your opinion, present reasons, support your reasons with evidence, and explain the significance of your supporting facts and ideas.

RESPOND TO THE PROMPT
- **Plan** by stating your opinion and listing reasons that support it. Select the strongest and most convincing reasons. Then identify facts, examples, and other details that back up each reason.
- **Draft** your response by stating your position, or thesis. Present your reasons from weakest to strongest or in another order that makes sense. Explain each reason using relevant details.
- **Revise** to use more precise wording, to vary sentences, to insert additional evidence, and to add transitions.
- **Edit** your writing to correct errors in spelling, grammar, punctuation, or capitalization.

Benchmark Composition: Persuasive Essay 1   Score Point 4

A Different Vision of Life

If you could, wouldn't you want to increase students' chances of getting into a top university or finding a good job? One way to do this is to increase their fluency in a second language. Two years of foreign-language study should be a graduation requirement for all seniors.

Many students avoid a language elective if they can take something easier. But this decision limits the universities or colleges to which they can apply. Some of the best universities require at least two years of a language other than English before they will even consider an application. Lots of students wait until their senior year in high school to think about college. By then, if they haven't studied another language, they've already lost the chance to enter some top universities.

However, it isn't just college-bound students who have narrowed their options. Many jobs require fluency in a second language, such as Spanish or Vietnamese. In some large cities, police officers and firefighters are paid more if they are fluent in languages spoken in the communities they serve. For example, bilingual police officers in Houston, Texas, receive a pay supplement for their language skills. Bilingual firefighters in Phoenix, Arizona, receive $100 extra per month. In a tight job market, it can be an advantage to know another language.

Studying the grammar, sentence structure, and vocabulary of another language also improves students' grasp of English. My father told me that he did not understand the subjunctive in English until he studied French. Similarly, my uncle Abraham said that studying Italian increased his English vocabulary.

Some people worry that if states require students to study a second language for two years, electives such as drama, band, and art will have to be eliminated. However, school officials just need to think outside the box. Many schools, including mine, have added a pre-school period for elective options. For example, I take orchestra in the early period. Students who want to learn a second language will simply have to get to school a little earlier.

Adding a second-language requirement will help prepare students to get into good colleges and to advance further in their jobs. Just as important, studying a second language will help us understand other cultures and be competitive in the modern world. Let's learn another language and become better citizens of the world—and of our own country.

DEVELOPMENT OF IDEAS
The first paragraph ends with a clear statement of the writer's position, or thesis—that students should be required to study a foreign language in order to graduate from high school.

DEVELOPMENT OF IDEAS
In the second and third paragraphs, the writer presents facts and examples that support the thesis. These details appeal to readers' logic.

ORGANIZATION/ PROGRESSION
Throughout the essay, the writer uses transitions that show the relationships between ideas.

DEVELOPMENT OF IDEAS
An objection that some readers might have is addressed in the fifth paragraph. The writer presents a solution to the opposing view that is supported by personal experience.

Persuasive Essay 1: Score Summary and Rubric   **Score Point 4**

This writer's language, evidence, and organization create a strongly persuasive argument. The tone is rational and balanced. The evidence includes many relevant facts and examples. The conclusion restates key reasons for a foreign-language requirement and expresses a commonly held belief: Americans need to be bilingual in a competitive world. There are no distracting errors.

	ORGANIZATION/ PROGRESSION	DEVELOPMENT OF IDEAS	USE OF LANGUAGE CONVENTIONS
4	• Uses an effective organization for a persuasive essay that is skillfully structured to suit the purpose, audience, and context • Conveys ideas in a sustained, persuasive way • Uses clear transitions between ideas, sentences, and paragraphs	• Advances a clear thesis or position fully supported by logical reasons and reliable, relevant evidence, including facts, expert opinions, and/or quotations • Presents a full range of relevant perspectives • Uses effective rhetorical devices and appeals to logic, emotions, and ethical beliefs	• Shows strong understanding of appropriate word choice for the form, purpose, and tone of a persuasive essay • Uses purposeful, varied, and controlled sentences • Demonstrates consistent command of conventions so that writing is fluent and clear
3	• Uses a reasonably effective organization for a persuasive essay, with a structure appropriate to the purpose, audience, and context • Conveys ideas in a fairly sustained, persuasive way • Uses transitions between ideas, sentences, and paragraphs	• Advances a fairly clear thesis or position supported by logical reasons and reliable, relevant evidence • Presents a range of relevant perspectives • Uses rhetorical devices and appeals to logic, emotions, and ethical beliefs	• Shows basic understanding of word choice appropriate for a persuasive essay • Uses sentences that are purposeful, varied, and controlled for the most part • Demonstrates a good command of conventions; writing is mostly fluent and clear
2	• Uses a somewhat effective organization for a persuasive essay that shows some attention to purpose, audience, and context • Does not convey all ideas in a sustained, persuasive way • Uses too few transitions between ideas, sentences, and paragraphs	• Has an unclear thesis or position statement; thesis is supported by insufficient reasons and evidence • Presents few relevant perspectives other than the author's • Uses few rhetorical devices or appeals to logic, emotions, and ethical beliefs	• Shows some understanding of word choice; may be inappropriate to form, purpose, or tone • May use awkward, rambling sentences or unvaried sentence structure • Demonstrates limited command of conventions, weakening fluency of writing
1	• Uses an ineffective organization for a persuasive essay • Does not convey ideas in a sustained, persuasive way • Has few or no transitions between ideas, sentences, and paragraphs	• Fails to state a thesis or support it with reasons and evidence • Fails to present other relevant perspectives • Uses few or no effective rhetorical devices or appeals to logic, emotions, and ethical beliefs	• Lacks appropriate word choice for form and purpose; has an inappropriate tone • Uses sentences that consistently lack purpose and control; sentence structure is monotonous • Demonstrates limited knowledge of conventions, resulting in a lack of fluency

Benchmark Composition: Persuasive Essay 1

Score Point 2

Enough Is Enough

I am truely apalled at the idea of adding something else that a student has to do to gradate. As if we dont have enough to do all ready. Two years of a forien langauge to get a diploma—some of us will still be in high school trying to pass when were 90! Vote this down or your gonna have some mighty mad students, me included. I all ready have a full shedule. Which is hard enough beleive me. When I roll in here in the AM I can hardly bare to look ahead to my day. I take six courses, which I need to pass all of them. Now your telling me I have to take some more. I cant. Its that simple. You maybe have gessed I am not the best student in the world. I spend all my time and energy just trying to pass what I am taking now. I cant do any more. Plus wear am I going to use another langauge. I dont know anyone who knows one. I all ready have my job for after high school. I probaly dont even need a diploma to work in my uncles factory. But I want one for my own pride. Your plan is going to take my pride away from me.

Think about why you want us to study a forien langauge. It is to make you look good or to really help us? If it is to help us than dont add this extra burden to our all ready stressed lifes.

ORGANIZATION/ PROGRESSION

The opening sentences clearly convey the writer's position on the issue. In addition, two distinct reasons are presented and explained. However, the lack of paragraph breaks makes it difficult to follow the argument.

USE OF LANGUAGE CONVENTIONS

Although the writer shows some good control of sentence structure in this essay, readers have to work hard to ignore or interpret the numerous misspellings.

Persuasive Essay 1: Score Summary and Rubric   **Score Point 2**

In spite of its flaws, such as poor spelling and inadequate paragraphing, this essay is persuasive. The writer feels strongly about the issue and presents two good reasons, as well as some support. The tone is passionate and engaging. The essay is weakened, however, by a failure to address opposing views.

	ORGANIZATION/ PROGRESSION	DEVELOPMENT OF IDEAS	USE OF LANGUAGE CONVENTIONS
4	• Uses an effective organization for a persuasive essay that is skillfully structured to suit the purpose, audience, and context • Conveys ideas in a sustained, persuasive way • Uses clear transitions between ideas, sentences, and paragraphs	• Advances a clear thesis or position fully supported by logical reasons and reliable, relevant evidence, including facts, expert opinions, and/or quotations • Presents a full range of relevant perspectives • Uses effective rhetorical devices and appeals to logic, emotions, and ethical beliefs	• Shows strong understanding of appropriate word choice for the form, purpose, and tone of a persuasive essay • Uses purposeful, varied, and controlled sentences • Demonstrates consistent command of conventions so that writing is fluent and clear
3	• Uses a reasonably effective organization for a persuasive essay, with a structure appropriate to the purpose, audience, and context • Conveys ideas in a fairly sustained, persuasive way • Uses transitions between ideas, sentences, and paragraphs	• Advances a fairly clear thesis or position supported by logical reasons and reliable, relevant evidence • Presents a range of relevant perspectives • Uses rhetorical devices and appeals to logic, emotions, and ethical beliefs	• Shows basic understanding of word choice appropriate for a persuasive essay • Uses sentences that are purposeful, varied, and controlled for the most part • Demonstrates a good command of conventions; writing is mostly fluent and clear
2	• Uses a somewhat effective organization for a persuasive essay that shows some attention to purpose, audience, and context • Does not convey all ideas in a sustained, persuasive way • Uses too few transitions between ideas, sentences, and paragraphs	• Has an unclear thesis or position statement; thesis is supported by insufficient reasons and evidence • Presents few relevant perspectives other than the author's • Uses few rhetorical devices or appeals to logic, emotions, and ethical beliefs	• Shows some understanding of word choice; may be inappropriate to form, purpose, or tone • May use awkward, rambling sentences or unvaried sentence structure • Demonstrates limited command of conventions, weakening fluency of writing
1	• Uses an ineffective organization for a persuasive essay • Does not convey ideas in a sustained, persuasive way • Has few or no transitions between ideas, sentences, and paragraphs	• Fails to state a thesis or support it with reasons and evidence • Fails to present other relevant perspectives • Uses few or no effective rhetorical devices or appeals to logic, emotions, and ethical beliefs	• Lacks appropriate word choice for form and purpose; has an inappropriate tone • Uses sentences that consistently lack purpose and control; sentence structure is monotonous • Demonstrates limited knowledge of conventions, resulting in a lack of fluency

Written Composition: Persuasive Essay 2

READ

Read the quotation in the box below.

> "It is not an arrogant government that chooses priorities, it's an irresponsible government that fails to choose."
>
> *Tony Blair*

THINK

There are many issues that demand a government's attention and resources. What do you think should be the top priority for your local, state, or national government? Why?

WRITE

Write an editorial for your local newspaper in which you persuade readers that your issue should be a priority for the government.

As you write your composition, remember to —

☐ state a thesis that identifies the issue that you think the government should focus on

☐ organize your argument logically and effectively, using transitions to show relationships between ideas

☐ develop your argument with strong reasons supported by relevant facts and other evidence, and use rhetorical devices to strengthen your argument

☐ make sure your composition is no longer than one page

TEKS 13A, 13B, 13C, 13D, 16A, 16B, 16C, 16F, 17, 18, 19

ANALYZE THE PROMPT

The prompt asks you to write an editorial in which you present an issue you think the government should focus on. You need to clearly state the issue and explain your reasons for choosing it.

RESPOND TO THE PROMPT

- **Plan** by listing problems or concerns facing your community, state, or nation. Choose the one that you feel is in most urgent need of attention. Then identify reasons, examples, facts, and other details that will help to convey your position to your audience.

- **Draft** your response by stating your position, or thesis. Present your reasons from weakest to strongest or in another order that makes sense. Explain each reason using relevant details.

- **Revise** to use more precise wording, to vary sentences, to insert additional explanation, and to add transitions.

- **Edit** your writing to correct errors in spelling, grammar, punctuation, or capitalization.

Name _____ Date _____

Benchmark Composition: Persuasive Essay 2   **Score Point 4**

The Ultimate Frontier

With the slashing of NASA budgets in Washington, the exploration of space as the last frontier now seems far-fetched. While the federal bureaucracy buries itself in worldly matters, the cutting edge of space and the atmosphere has been left to European powers and privatized aerospace corporations. We Americans need to get our priorities back in order and complete what we started in space in order to reap the big benefits that could result.

Even as I write this editorial, Earth's atmosphere is deteriorating and the environment is under assault. We are overcrowded and running out of natural resources. Investigation and research have shown that there is a very good chance of finding energy, minerals, and other resources in space, if we continue our efforts to explore and map our universe. It is "penny wise" and "pound foolish" to stop programs now and have to start all over again in the future.

In addition, the space race has led to unprecedented leaps in our technical and scientific knowledge. For example, we have a 123,000-miles-per-hour plasma engine proficient enough to reach Mars in 39 days. That is 33,550,540 miles in just over a month! We have spacesuits that allow humans to breathe inside a vacuum for an extended period of time. We have space vehicles with state-of-the-art safety measures. While not all of these advances directly help those of us earthbound, many do. New technologies learned from the space program make our cars safer, even if we are not going to rack up millions of miles. Medicine has advanced thanks to materials proven beneficial in space.

Of course, why spend government money when private corporations are taking up the slack? Already Virgin Airlines has developed aerospace crafts capable of carrying civilians to the outer edges of the atmosphere, effectively creating a tourism industry in space. But if these corporations succeed in plumbing the mysteries of the universe, who exactly will own rights in space? Will its commodities be sold to the highest bidder? Instead of serving the common good, it is foreseeable in this scenario that space will serve only the wealthy.

As taxpayers, it is up to us to lobby government officials to continue investing in our future. And space is our future. It holds the promise of solutions to many of our problems and will yield the increase of knowledge, which can only enrich all of us. Say to your representative, "We want to go into the wild blue yonder!"

DEVELOPMENT OF IDEAS
The introduction includes background information about the issue that the writer is going to address and ends with a clear thesis statement that leads into the body of the editorial.

ORGANIZATION/ PROGRESSION
Frequent use of transitions helps readers follow the writer's argument, signaling the major reasons and supporting evidence.

DEVELOPMENT OF IDEAS
In the third paragraph, the writer develops the central argument with facts and specific examples of ways that everyone benefits from space exploration.

DEVELOPMENT OF IDEAS
In the fourth paragraph, the writer uses rhetorical questions to identify an opposing view and present a response to it. This device catches readers' attention while bolstering the strength of the argument.

Persuasive Essay 2: Score Summary and Rubric   **Score Point 4**

The strength of this editorial lies in its organization. The writer presents two strong reasons and a counterargument backed up by relevant evidence. All details are relevant to the thesis. The tone of the writer is appropriately serious but also engaging *(even if we are not going to rack up millions of miles)*. There are no distracting errors.

	ORGANIZATION/ PROGRESSION	DEVELOPMENT OF IDEAS	USE OF LANGUAGE CONVENTIONS
4	• Uses an effective organization for a persuasive essay that is skillfully structured to suit the purpose, audience, and context • Conveys ideas in a sustained, persuasive way • Uses clear transitions between ideas, sentences, and paragraphs	• Advances a clear thesis or position fully supported by logical reasons and reliable, relevant evidence, including facts, expert opinions, and/or quotations • Presents a full range of relevant perspectives • Uses effective rhetorical devices and appeals to logic, emotions, and ethical beliefs	• Shows strong understanding of appropriate word choice for the form, purpose, and tone of a persuasive essay • Uses purposeful, varied, and controlled sentences • Demonstrates consistent command of conventions so that writing is fluent and clear
3	• Uses a reasonably effective organization for a persuasive essay, with a structure appropriate to the purpose, audience, and context • Conveys ideas in a fairly sustained, persuasive way • Uses transitions between ideas, sentences, and paragraphs	• Advances a fairly clear thesis or position supported by logical reasons and reliable, relevant evidence • Presents a range of relevant perspectives • Uses rhetorical devices and appeals to logic, emotions, and ethical beliefs	• Shows basic understanding of word choice appropriate for a persuasive essay • Uses sentences that are purposeful, varied, and controlled for the most part • Demonstrates a good command of conventions; writing is mostly fluent and clear
2	• Uses a somewhat effective organization for a persuasive essay that shows some attention to purpose, audience, and context • Does not convey all ideas in a sustained, persuasive way • Uses too few transitions between ideas, sentences, and paragraphs	• Has an unclear thesis or position statement; thesis is supported by insufficient reasons and evidence • Presents few relevant perspectives other than the author's • Uses few rhetorical devices or appeals to logic, emotions, and ethical beliefs	• Shows some understanding of word choice; may be inappropriate to form, purpose, or tone • May use awkward, rambling sentences or unvaried sentence structure • Demonstrates limited command of conventions, weakening fluency of writing
1	• Uses an ineffective organization for a persuasive essay • Does not convey ideas in a sustained, persuasive way • Has few or no transitions between ideas, sentences, and paragraphs	• Fails to state a thesis or support it with reasons and evidence • Fails to present other relevant perspectives • Uses few or no effective rhetorical devices or appeals to logic, emotions, and ethical beliefs	• Lacks appropriate word choice for form and purpose; has an inappropriate tone • Uses sentences that consistently lack purpose and control; sentence structure is monotonous • Demonstrates limited knowledge of conventions, resulting in a lack of fluency

Benchmark Composition: Persuasive Essay 2

Score Point 2

Save Our Seniors

Senior citizens are in trouble in our country. My grandmother does not have a lot of money. She makes it stretch. For example, she buys a whole chicken. She eats the chicken. Then she makes soup with the bones and eats that. She lives in a small apartment. She worked all her life and saved too. But after she pays her bills she has not that much left over. The government needs to help senior citizens more. They make things very confusing. My grandmother did not get some money. Because they said she filled out a form wrong. They need to have more people help seniors with paperwork. There need to be more programs. For example, my grandmother sometimes does not have enough money to turn her heat up. Why should seniors suffer? Give them breaks on heating bills. Give them breaks on medicine. There are some programs to help senior citizens with medicine. But not enough. Plus they are confusing too.

In conclusion, I say the government needs to put senior citizens first. After all we are all going to be old someday. So helping old people now is helping all of us later.

ORGANIZATION/ PROGRESSION

The editorial is weakened by the position of the thesis statement in the center of the essay rather than at the beginning, where it would have provided a focus. Although several transitions are used, they are not effective in connecting the ideas to the major reasons.

USE OF LANGUAGE CONVENTIONS

The writer's spelling, vocabulary, and fundamental sentence structure are sound with the exception of a few fragments and unclear pronoun references.

Name _____ Date _____

In this editorial, the writer advances a clear thesis *(The government needs to help senior citizens more).* Relevant observations and examples drawn from the writer's experience support the thesis. However, a lack of organization undermines the essay's effectiveness. The writer's failure to order reasons and evidence logically makes the argument difficult to follow and evaluate.

	ORGANIZATION/ PROGRESSION	DEVELOPMENT OF IDEAS	USE OF LANGUAGE CONVENTIONS
4	• Uses an effective organization for a persuasive essay that is skillfully structured to suit the purpose, audience, and context • Conveys ideas in a sustained, persuasive way • Uses clear transitions between ideas, sentences, and paragraphs	• Advances a clear thesis or position fully supported by logical reasons and reliable, relevant evidence, including facts, expert opinions, and/or quotations • Presents a full range of relevant perspectives • Uses effective rhetorical devices and appeals to logic, emotions, and ethical beliefs	• Shows strong understanding of appropriate word choice for the form, purpose, and tone of a persuasive essay • Uses purposeful, varied, and controlled sentences • Demonstrates consistent command of conventions so that writing is fluent and clear
3	• Uses a reasonably effective organization for a persuasive essay, with a structure appropriate to the purpose, audience, and context • Conveys ideas in a fairly sustained, persuasive way • Uses transitions between ideas, sentences, and paragraphs	• Advances a fairly clear thesis or position supported by logical reasons and reliable, relevant evidence • Presents a range of relevant perspectives • Uses rhetorical devices and appeals to logic, emotions, and ethical beliefs	• Shows basic understanding of word choice appropriate for a persuasive essay • Uses sentences that are purposeful, varied, and controlled for the most part • Demonstrates a good command of conventions; writing is mostly fluent and clear
2	• Uses a somewhat effective organization for a persuasive essay that shows some attention to purpose, audience, and context • Does not convey all ideas in a sustained, persuasive way • Uses too few transitions between ideas, sentences, and paragraphs	• Has an unclear thesis or position statement; thesis is supported by insufficient reasons and evidence • Presents few relevant perspectives other than the author's • Uses few rhetorical devices or appeals to logic, emotions, and ethical beliefs	• Shows some understanding of word choice; may be inappropriate to form, purpose, or tone • May use awkward, rambling sentences or unvaried sentence structure • Demonstrates limited command of conventions, weakening fluency of writing
1	• Uses an ineffective organization for a persuasive essay • Does not convey ideas in a sustained, persuasive way • Has few or no transitions between ideas, sentences, and paragraphs	• Fails to state a thesis or support it with reasons and evidence • Fails to present other relevant perspectives • Uses few or no effective rhetorical devices or appeals to logic, emotions, and ethical beliefs	• Lacks appropriate word choice for form and purpose; has an inappropriate tone • Uses sentences that consistently lack purpose and control; sentence structure is monotonous • Demonstrates limited knowledge of conventions, resulting in a lack of fluency

Written Composition: Analytical Essay 1

READ

Read the poem in the box below.

I never hear the word "escape"

I never hear the word "escape"
Without a quicker blood,
A sudden expectation,
A flying attitude!

I never heard of prisons broad
By soldiers battered down,
But I tug childish at my bars,
Only to fail again!

Emily Dickinson

THINK

Poets choose words and images to create certain effects.

WRITE

Write an essay that analyzes how the words and images in this poem emphasize the idea of escape.

As you write your composition, remember to —

☐ craft a thesis statement that explains how the poem's language emphasizes the idea of escape

☐ organize your ideas in a logical order and connect them with appropriate transitions

☐ support your analysis with references to the text as well as direct quotations

☐ make sure your composition is no longer than one page

TEKS 13A, 13B, 13C, 13D, 15A, 17, 18, 19

ANALYZE THE PROMPT

The prompt asks you to think about how the language in the poem conveys the poet's meaning. Therefore, you must state what idea the poet wishes to convey about escape and then show how the words and images bring out this idea.

RESPOND TO THE PROMPT

- **Plan** by identifying the words and phrases in the poem that convey an attitude toward the concept of escape. Jot down ideas about what each example contributes. Summarize the speaker's overall view of escape.
- **Draft** your response by writing an introduction stating your thesis. Then write one or more paragraphs that support your thesis with details and examples. End with a conclusion that restates your thesis in a powerful way.
- **Revise** to use more precise wording, to vary sentences, and to add transitions.
- **Edit** your essay to correct errors in spelling, grammar, punctuation, and capitalization.

Benchmark Composition: Analytical Essay 1

Escape

This poem, so deceptively simple as to appear almost simplistic, delivers a subtle message about the idea of escape and human nature through the juxtaposition of two very different ideas. In the first stanza, the speaker seems imminently poised to leave a place, but in the second stanza, the language and images make it clear that the speaker is going nowhere.

The poem opens with exhilaration, the first four lines spilling over with words that show the speaker's excited reaction to the idea of "escape." The speaker's blood runs "quicker." There is a "sudden expectation," a "flying attitude." All of these words convey anticipation and urgency at the thought of attaining the freedom that comes from leaving one's old life and starting fresh. They create a mental image of the suddenness with which a bird takes flight—on a whim, without baggage, spontaneously. Through this language, the shortness of the lines, and the images evoked, the poet creates momentum that reinforces the impression of the speaker's strong desire to escape.

In the second stanza, however, the language changes. The words themselves as well as the lines that contain them become weightier, slower, and more ponderous. "Prisons broad" and "soldiers battered down" deepen the sense of futility that permeates the latter half of the poem as the speaker tries to escape "only to fail again." Yet the description of the speaker's attempt as "childish" suggests that the speaker is half-hearted about making the escape, while at the same time lamenting the failure to do so.

Through these distinctly different halves of the poem, Dickinson seems to be suggesting while we may dream of escape or a fresh start, at the same time we cling to what holds us in place—our bars. And so, the paradox that is human nature continues—wanting to go yet needing to stay, a conflict made more intense by our inability to resolve it.

ORGANIZATION/ PROGRESSION
The introductory paragraph offers an insight on the overall theme of the poem before stating the thesis that identifies how this theme is brought out.

DEVELOPMENT OF IDEAS
In the body paragraphs, the writer supports each analytical or interpretative statement with words and phrases quoted from the poem.

DEVELOPMENT OF IDEAS
In both the second and the third paragraphs, the last sentence explains the significance of the ideas presented and draws a conclusion that helps readers understand what they have just read.

DEVELOPMENT OF IDEAS
The conclusion relates back to the introduction, showing how the images and language in both stanzas combine to convey one theme about escape and human nature.

Analytical Essay 1: Score Summary and Rubric　　　　　　　　　　Score Point 4

This analytical essay shows a deep understanding of Dickinson's poem and an ability to present these insights clearly and coherently. The writer explains the relevance of Dickinson's message, relating it to a common facet of human nature. An accessible style engages the audience.

	ORGANIZATION/ PROGRESSION	DEVELOPMENT OF IDEAS	USE OF LANGUAGE CONVENTIONS
4	• Uses appropriate structure and organization for analytical response • Includes introductory and concluding paragraphs • Advances thesis statement that establishes unity and focus • Controls progression with transitions showing relationships among ideas	• Supports thesis with substantial text evidence and commentary • Analyzes use of rhetorical devices, stylistic elements, and complexities in text • Engages the reader through thoughtful development of ideas; demonstrates a deep understanding of text	• Shows understanding of word choice appropriate to purpose and intended tone • Uses purposeful, varied, and controlled sentences • Adds interest to writing with use of tropes, schemes, and other rhetorical devices • Demonstrates a command of conventions
3	• Uses mostly effective structure for purpose and demands of analytical response • Includes introductory and concluding ideas • Relates most ideas to thesis; essay is coherent though may lack overall unity • Mostly controls progression of ideas with transitions	• Supports thesis with specific, appropriate details, including references to text • Provides analysis of some rhetorical devices, stylistic elements, and complexities in text • Demonstrates some depth of thought; shows a good understanding of the text	• Shows a basic understanding of word choice, appropriate to purpose and tone • Uses varied and generally controlled sentences • Employs some rhetorical devices • Demonstrates general command of conventions; errors do not seriously affect clarity or fluency
2	• May use structure that is inappropriate for analytical essay • Has undeveloped introduction and/or conclusion • May use weak or unclear thesis • Has inconsistent progression of thought, with too few meaningful transitions	• Supports ideas cursorily with little relevant evidence; includes few text references • Provides superficial or inaccurate analysis of text elements • Demonstrates limited understanding of the text, little depth of thought, and a formulaic response	• Shows limited grasp of word choice; fails to establish appropriate tone • Uses uncontrolled or awkward sentences • Expresses ideas simplistically • Demonstrates partial command of conventions; errors may result in a lack of fluency or clarity
1	• Uses inappropriate or no obvious structure • Lacks introduction and conclusion • Lacks clear thesis, with resulting weak focus and coherence • Has weak progression of thought, with few meaningful transitions	• Includes few relevant details; lacks textual references • Provides inadequate analysis of text • Demonstrates lack of understanding of text through confused or vague approach	• Lacks understanding of word choice; vocabulary is imprecise or unsuitable • Uses simplistic, awkward, or uncontrolled sentences • Demonstrates limited or no command of conventions, resulting in a lack of fluency

Benchmark Composition: Analytical Essay 1

Score Point 2

Fear of Flying

The author feels like she needs to get out of there, like this place is not for her. "Escape" could be talking about her home, her school, or an actual jail. Anyone sitting in one of those places who hears someone use the word "escape" would want out, just as the author says she does. But she can't. She feels like a helpless little kid who has to ask grownups to do things for her, because all she can do is "tug childish" on her prison bars. When you picture someone tugging childishly, they are powerless and small, unable to do anything for themselves. I can relate. Last year I had a broken leg. I was pretty helpless. People had to carry my books and even open doors for me. I would stand there on my crutches, "childish." This makes me wonder if the poet was handicapped or crippled in some kind of way. Even if she isn't crippled in reality, she feels crippled, because the idea of flying makes her heart beat faster. Or, maybe she is afraid of flying!

ORGANIZATION/ PROGRESSION

Instead of crafting an introduction with a unifying thesis statement, the writer simply launches into an explanation of the first stanza. Just as abruptly, the focus then shifts to the second stanza with no transitional words to guide readers' understanding.

USE OF LANGUAGE CONVENTIONS

The sentences in this essay are well-structured and controlled. The writer shows a good grasp of spelling.

Name _____ Date _____

The writer's skillful use of conventions masks some of the errors in logic and organization. The interpretation of the language in the poem is accurate. However, the lack of an introduction, conclusion, or thesis and the inclusion of extraneous details weakens the essay's overall impact.

	ORGANIZATION/ PROGRESSION	DEVELOPMENT OF IDEAS	USE OF LANGUAGE CONVENTIONS
4	• Uses appropriate structure and organization for analytical response • Includes introductory and concluding paragraphs • Advances thesis statement that establishes unity and focus • Controls progression with transitions showing relationships among ideas	• Supports thesis with substantial text evidence and commentary • Analyzes use of rhetorical devices, stylistic elements, and complexities in text • Engages the reader through thoughtful development of ideas; demonstrates a deep understanding of text	• Shows understanding of word choice appropriate to purpose and intended tone • Uses purposeful, varied, and controlled sentences • Adds interest to writing with use of tropes, schemes, and other rhetorical devices • Demonstrates a command of conventions
3	• Uses mostly effective structure for purpose and demands of analytical response • Includes introductory and concluding ideas • Relates most ideas to thesis; essay is coherent though may lack overall unity • Mostly controls progression of ideas with transitions	• Supports thesis with specific, appropriate details, including references to text • Provides analysis of some rhetorical devices, stylistic elements, and complexities in text • Demonstrates some depth of thought; shows a good understanding of the text	• Shows a basic understanding of word choice, appropriate to purpose and tone • Uses varied and generally controlled sentences • Employs some rhetorical devices • Demonstrates general command of conventions; errors do not seriously affect clarity or fluency
2	• May use structure that is inappropriate for analytical essay • Has undeveloped introduction and/or conclusion • May use weak or unclear thesis • Has inconsistent progression of thought, with too few meaningful transitions	• Supports ideas cursorily with little relevant evidence; includes few text references • Provides superficial or inaccurate analysis of text elements • Demonstrates limited understanding of the text, little depth of thought, and a formulaic response	• Shows limited grasp of word choice; fails to establish appropriate tone • Uses uncontrolled or awkward sentences • Expresses ideas simplistically • Demonstrates partial command of conventions; errors may result in a lack of fluency or clarity
1	• Uses inappropriate or no obvious structure • Lacks introduction and conclusion • Lacks clear thesis, with resulting weak focus and coherence • Has weak progression of thought, with few meaningful transitions	• Includes few relevant details; lacks textual references • Provides inadequate analysis of text • Demonstrates lack of understanding of text through confused or vague approach	• Lacks understanding of word choice; vocabulary is imprecise or unsuitable • Uses simplistic, awkward, or uncontrolled sentences • Demonstrates limited or no command of conventions, resulting in a lack of fluency

Written Composition: Analytical Essay 2

READ

Read the passage in the box below.

> There is a solid bottom everywhere. We read that the traveler asked the boy if the swamp before him had a hard bottom. The boy replied that it had. But presently the traveler's horse sank in up to the girths, and he observed to the boy, "I thought you said that this bog had a hard bottom." "So it has," answered the latter, "but you have not got half way to it yet."
>
> *Henry David Thoreau,* Walden

ANALYZE THE PROMPT
The prompt asks you to explain how Thoreau's message about finding truth is conveyed through the anecdote that he presents.

THINK

To convey their meanings, writers sometimes use anecdotes. These are brief stories that illustrate a point.

WRITE

Write an essay that explains how Thoreau's use of the anecdote in this passage shows the importance of finding truth in our lives.

RESPOND TO THE PROMPT
- **Plan** by jotting down details of your interpretation of the anecdote's meaning, keeping in mind that it relates to the idea of finding the truth.
- **Draft** your response by writing an introduction that states your thesis. Then write one or more paragraphs that support your thesis with details and examples. End with a conclusion that restates your thesis in a powerful way.
- **Revise** to use more precise wording, to vary sentences, and to add transitions.
- **Edit** your essay to correct errors in spelling, grammar, punctuation, and capitalization.

As you write your composition, remember to —

☐ develop a thesis statement that explains how the anecdote reveals Thoreau's idea about finding truth

☐ organize your ideas in a logical order and connect them with appropriate transitions

☐ support your analysis with commentary on the text as well as direct quotations

☐ make sure your composition is no longer than one page

TEKS 13A, 13B, 13C, 13D, 15A, 17, 18, 19

Name _____ Date _____

Benchmark Composition: Analytical Essay 2

Seeking the Truth

Thoreau's sojourn on Walden Pond afforded him the time and the opportunity to reflect on the meaning of life and the best way to go about living it. This excerpt, from his book Walden, conveys one of his insights through an anecdote that illustrates the importance of finding truth in our lives.

The anecdote, humorous in its gentle irony, tells of a traveler who asks whether a swamp has a solid bottom. A boy replies that it does. When the horse becomes mired in the bog, the traveler believes the boy has misled him—that there really is not a solid bottom. But the boy says that the horse has "not got half way to it yet."

Thoreau uses this anecdote to symbolize what occurs in many people's lives. As they search for what gives life meaning, or the truth, they get bogged down. They lose sight of what is essential and real; they are sidetracked by other concerns, such as the pursuit of material gain, that obscure what should be their true priorities. They flounder and question whether life has any meaning at all.

But "there is a solid bottom everywhere." Through this anecdote, Thoreau is counseling that with patience, deliberation, and persistence, we can all locate it. We must not give up and become discouraged when we are only halfway there. We also must not settle for less than solid ground; otherwise we will spend the rest of our lives wading through the mire and accomplishing nothing. Our truth, like a firm surface, will enable us to advance confidently and smoothly toward our destination.

Thoreau went to the woods to discover his truth. We can benefit from his experience and follow his direction to help us discover ours.

ORGANIZATION/ PROGRESSION
The first sentence of the essay provides an introduction to the author and a brief context for the essay's central idea.

DEVELOPMENT OF IDEAS
In the second paragraph, the writer briefly summarizes the anecdote, giving readers all the information they need to understand the subsequent analysis of its meaning.

DEVELOPMENT OF IDEAS
The third and fourth paragraphs present an interpretation of the anecdote's deeper meaning, supported by references to the text.

ORGANIZATION/ PROGRESSION
The conclusion makes clear the relevance of Thoreau's lesson to contemporary readers.

Name _____ Date _____

This analytical essay, while short, develops a thorough response to the prompt, incorporating quotations and getting to the heart of the anecdote's meaning. The writer's vocabulary and command of sentence structure create a discussion that is at once sophisticated and engaging.

	ORGANIZATION/ PROGRESSION	DEVELOPMENT OF IDEAS	USE OF LANGUAGE CONVENTIONS
4	• Uses appropriate structure and organization for analytical response • Includes introductory and concluding paragraphs • Advances thesis statement that establishes unity and focus • Controls progression with transitions showing relationships among ideas	• Supports thesis with substantial text evidence and commentary • Analyzes use of rhetorical devices, stylistic elements, and complexities in text • Engages the reader through thoughtful development of ideas; demonstrates a deep understanding of text	• Shows understanding of word choice appropriate to purpose and intended tone • Uses purposeful, varied, and controlled sentences • Adds interest to writing with use of tropes, schemes, and other rhetorical devices • Demonstrates a command of conventions
3	• Uses mostly effective structure for purpose and demands of analytical response • Includes introductory and concluding ideas • Relates most ideas to thesis; essay is coherent though may lack overall unity • Mostly controls progression of ideas with transitions	• Supports thesis with specific, appropriate details, including references to text • Provides analysis of some rhetorical devices, stylistic elements, and complexities in text • Demonstrates some depth of thought; shows a good understanding of the text	• Shows a basic understanding of word choice, appropriate to purpose and tone • Uses varied and generally controlled sentences • Employs some rhetorical devices • Demonstrates general command of conventions; errors do not seriously affect clarity or fluency
2	• May use structure that is inappropriate for analytical essay • Has undeveloped introduction and/or conclusion • May use weak or unclear thesis • Has inconsistent progression of thought, with too few meaningful transitions	• Supports ideas cursorily with little relevant evidence; includes few text references • Provides superficial or inaccurate analysis of text elements • Demonstrates limited understanding of the text, little depth of thought, and a formulaic response	• Shows limited grasp of word choice; fails to establish appropriate tone • Uses uncontrolled or awkward sentences • Expresses ideas simplistically • Demonstrates partial command of conventions; errors may result in a lack of fluency or clarity
1	• Uses inappropriate or no obvious structure • Lacks introduction and conclusion • Lacks clear thesis, with resulting weak focus and coherence • Has weak progression of thought, with few meaningful transitions	• Includes few relevant details; lacks textual references • Provides inadequate analysis of text • Demonstrates lack of understanding of text through confused or vague approach	• Lacks understanding of word choice; vocabulary is imprecise or unsuitable • Uses simplistic, awkward, or uncontrolled sentences • Demonstrates limited or no command of conventions, resulting in a lack of fluency

Benchmark Composition: Analytical Essay 2

Thoreau and Lies

Thoreau lived on Walden Pond for a long time. He probably knew all about swamps from the pond. When it rained it was probably swampy. Maybe even his horse got stuck sometimes. Although I don't think he had one on Walden Pond. He wanted to live simple. I know this. We've already studied Thoreau in school. But he tells this story. I might start telling it too. It is about a horse getting stuck. The horse can't find the bottom of the swamp. Thoreau says there is always a bottom. But sometimes the bottom isn't easy to find. I guess the bottom is supposed to be the truth. The mud on top is maybe lies. Like that other saying that talks about how lies get you all tangled up. Thoreau is saying that lies suck you down and get you stuck. That is probably true. I have been stuck in a lie before. Once I told my best friend that I had to babysit my brother. But I was going to the mall with another friend. That my best friend didn't like. I knew she would be mad. But then my best friend told me she was going to the mall. So I ended up having to stay home. Or else my best friend would have seen me. She might not have been my best friend any more. If I had told the truth. I could have gone to the mall. I was bored! So in conclusion I think Thoreau is right. We need to tell the truth or we will be stuck in a swamp that we make ourselves just like that old horse.

DEVELOPMENT OF IDEAS
Although this essay lacks a thesis statement, the ideas are presented fairly logically. The writer describes the events in the anecdote and interprets them for readers. The writer's personal story may seem irrelevant, but it illustrates her interpretation of Thoreau's meaning well. The last sentence neatly summarizes the main idea.

USE OF LANGUAGE CONVENTIONS
Sentence structure is a major problem in this essay. Many sentence fragments mar the flow of the writing and make it more difficult for readers to follow the analysis.

Analytical Essay 2: Score Summary and Rubric   **Score Point 2**

This essay presents a meaningful analysis of the excerpt, supported by specific details from the text as well as the writer's own experiences. The absence of an introduction and a conclusion and the presence of sentence fragments weaken the essay's coherence.

	ORGANIZATION/ PROGRESSION	DEVELOPMENT OF IDEAS	USE OF LANGUAGE CONVENTIONS
4	• Uses appropriate structure and organization for analytical response • Includes introductory and concluding paragraphs • Advances thesis statement that establishes unity and focus • Controls progression with transitions showing relationships among ideas	• Supports thesis with substantial text evidence and commentary • Analyzes use of rhetorical devices, stylistic elements, and complexities in text • Engages the reader through thoughtful development of ideas; demonstrates a deep understanding of text	• Shows understanding of word choice appropriate to purpose and intended tone • Uses purposeful, varied, and controlled sentences • Adds interest to writing with use of tropes, schemes, and other rhetorical devices • Demonstrates a command of conventions
3	• Uses mostly effective structure for purpose and demands of analytical response • Includes introductory and concluding ideas • Relates most ideas to thesis; essay is coherent though may lack overall unity • Mostly controls progression of ideas with transitions	• Supports thesis with specific, appropriate details, including references to text • Provides analysis of some rhetorical devices, stylistic elements, and complexities in text • Demonstrates some depth of thought; shows a good understanding of the text	• Shows a basic understanding of word choice, appropriate to purpose and tone • Uses varied and generally controlled sentences • Employs some rhetorical devices • Demonstrates general command of conventions; errors do not seriously affect clarity or fluency
2	• May use structure that is inappropriate for analytical essay • Has undeveloped introduction and/or conclusion • May use weak or unclear thesis • Has inconsistent progression of thought, with too few meaningful transitions	• Supports ideas cursorily with little relevant evidence; includes few text references • Provides superficial or inaccurate analysis of text elements • Demonstrates limited understanding of the text, little depth of thought, and a formulaic response	• Shows limited grasp of word choice; fails to establish appropriate tone • Uses uncontrolled or awkward sentences • Expresses ideas simplistically • Demonstrates partial command of conventions; errors may result in a lack of fluency or clarity
1	• Uses inappropriate or no obvious structure • Lacks introduction and conclusion • Lacks clear thesis, with resulting weak focus and coherence • Has weak progression of thought, with few meaningful transitions	• Includes few relevant details; lacks textual references • Provides inadequate analysis of text • Demonstrates lack of understanding of text through confused or vague approach	• Lacks understanding of word choice; vocabulary is imprecise or unsuitable • Uses simplistic, awkward, or uncontrolled sentences • Demonstrates limited or no command of conventions, resulting in a lack of fluency

Written Composition Practice: Persuasive Essay 1

READ

Read the quotation in the box below.

> "Life be not so short but that there is always time for courtesy."
>
> *Ralph Waldo Emerson*

THINK

Manners, including holding the door open for others and saying "please" and "thank you," were once an integral part of people's interactions with each other. Increasingly, these outward signs of courtesy are being discarded. Are manners necessary in society, or do they just slow people down? Consider how courtesy, or the lack of it, affects you and the people you interact with.

WRITE

Write a persuasive essay addressed to the members of your English language arts class in which you argue why manners are or are not important in our daily lives.

As you write your composition, remember to —

☐ craft a thesis that clearly states your position on the importance of manners

☐ organize your argument logically and effectively, using transitions to show relationships between ideas

☐ develop your argument with strong reasons supported by relevant facts and other evidence, and use rhetorical devices to strengthen your argument

☐ make sure your composition is no longer than one page

Written Composition Practice: Persuasive Essay 2

READ

Read the quotation in the box below.

> "Those who expect moments of change to be comfortable and free of conflict have not learned their history."
>
> *Joan Wallach Scott*

THINK

Although change may be feared and resisted, it often brings about improvement. What change would you like to see implemented in your school, your local community, or an organization to which you belong? What would be the effects of this change?

WRITE

Write a speech for the audience most affected by your proposal in which you persuade your audience to accept your idea for a change.

As you write your composition, remember to —

☐ craft a thesis that clearly states what you would like to change and why

☐ organize your argument logically and effectively, using transitions to show relationships between ideas

☐ develop your argument with strong reasons supported by relevant facts and other evidence, and use rhetorical devices to strengthen your argument

☐ make sure your composition is no longer than one page

Written Composition Practice: Analytical Essay 1

READ

Read the poem in the box below.

Velvet Shoes

Let us walk in the white snow   We shall walk through the still town
    In a soundless space;   In a windless peace;
With footsteps quiet and slow,   We shall step upon white down,
    At a tranquil pace,   Upon silver fleece,
    Under veils of white lace.   Upon softer than these.

I shall go shod in silk,   We shall walk in velvet shoes:
    And you in wool,   Wherever we go
White as a white cow's milk,   Silence will fall like dews
    More beautiful   On white silence below.
    Than the breast of a gull.   We shall walk in the snow.

Elinor Wylie

THINK

The mood of a poem is the feeling or atmosphere that is created by the use of literary devices (such as imagery and figurative language), rhythm, and the sound of the words.

WRITE

Write an essay that explains how the sound of this poem and its literary devices produce a peaceful or serene mood.

As you write your composition, remember to —

☐ develop a thesis statement that explains how the poet's use of sound and literary devices contributes to the prevailing mood of peace

☐ organize your ideas in a logical order and connect them with appropriate transitions

☐ support your analysis with references to the text as well as direct quotations

☐ make sure your composition is no longer than one page

Written Composition Practice: Analytical Essay 2

READ

Read this excerpt from Chief Joseph's speech given in Washington, D.C., in 1879. The speech was delivered after Chief Joseph's people, the Nez Perce, were defeated in battle and removed from their land.

> I have heard talk and talk, but nothing is done. Good words do not last long unless they amount to something. Words do not pay for my dead people. They do not pay for my country, now overrun by white men. They do not protect my father's grave. They do not pay for all my horses and cattle. Good words will not give me back my children. Good words will not make good the promise of your War Chief General Miles. Good words will not give my people good health and stop them from dying. Good words will not get my people a home where they can live in peace and take care of themselves. I am tired of talk that comes to nothing.

THINK

Effective speakers use rhetorical devices such as repetition and parallelism.

WRITE

Write an essay that explains how the rhetorical devices used by Chief Joseph emphasize his meaning.

As you write your composition, remember to —

☐ develop a thesis statement that explains how Chief Joseph uses rhetorical devices effectively to convey his meaning

☐ organize your ideas in a logical order and connect them with appropriate transitions

☐ support your analysis with references to the text as well as direct quotations

☐ make sure your composition is no longer than one page

Revising and Editing

Guided Revising

Read the following persuasive essay. Then read each question and mark the correct answer.

Charlotte wrote this persuasive essay about the use of energy-efficient appliances. She would like you to read her essay and think about the improvements she should make. When you finish reading, answer the questions that follow.

Saving Energy Saves Money

(1) Every time you turn on a light, watch television, or do a load of laundry, you are polluting the planet. (2) This is because the energy used in our homes comes from power plants, which burn fossil fuels to create electricity. (3) Many of the appliances we take for granted use large amounts of electricity, enough so that the average home actually causes more pollution than the average car. (4) When we purchase energy-efficient appliances, we can reduce our carbon footprint. (5) We can also assure a long future for our planet.

(6) Some families think that they cannot make a difference and that their decisions do not matter. (7) For example, replacing a 20-year-old refrigerator with a new Energy Star–rated model will reduce your home's CO_2 production by about one ton per year. (8) Similarly, if every room air conditioner sold in the United States were Energy Star qualified, it would prevent 1.3 billion pounds of greenhouse emissions—the equivalent emissions from 115,000 cars. (9) By purchasing an Energy Star washing machine, a family could cut the energy costs of this appliance by a third and water costs by half.

(10) Some argue that energy-efficient appliances are simply too expensive for most families. (11) However, in the long run, by saving energy money is saved. (12) For most American families, ten to fifty percent of the money spent on energy is wasted due to inefficiency. (13) Proponents of energy-efficient appliances suggest that you think of your appliance as having two price tags: one is the price you pay at the store and the other is the price you pay to run the appliance. (14) Store prices for a single appliance can vary by several hundred dollars. (15) For example, replacing an old refrigerator with an energy-efficient model can save you $100 a year in energy costs, and replacing a pre-1994 dishwasher can save $110 a year. (16) If you multiply these savings by the life span of the appliance (10 to 20 years), the long-range savings more than pay for the initial high price tag.

(17) We all agree that we would like to make the planet a better place for ourselves and for our children. (18) Start to do your part today by urging your family, friends, and relatives to purchase only Energy Star appliances.

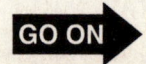

1 Charlotte wants to end her first paragraph with a clearly stated claim. What is the most effective way for her to rewrite sentences 4 and 5?

A If we want to reduce our carbon footprint, we should either purchase energy-efficient appliances or assure our planet a long future.

B If only energy-efficient appliances are purchased, our carbon footprint will be reduced, and a better future for our planet is assured.

C We all want our planet to have a long future, which is why we should purchase energy-efficient appliances and let our carbon footprint reduce.

D By purchasing only energy-efficient appliances, we can go a long way toward reducing our carbon footprint and assuring a better future for our planet.

> **EXPLANATION:** Charlotte's claim is that energy-efficient appliances will reduce pollution and help the planet. The correct answer is **D** because it is the clearest and most direct statement of her claim.
> - **A** is incorrect. The two outcomes of using energy-efficient appliances go together; the result is not an *either-or* relationship.
> - **B** is incorrect. Using passive verb forms (*are purchased, will be reduced, is assured*) rather than active ones weakens the claim.
> - **C** is incorrect. The relative clause beginning with "which is why" does not state the claim directly and forcefully. The phrase "let our carbon footprint reduce" is awkward.

TEKS 13C

2 To better engage her readers and show a contrast between ideas, what is the most effective way for Charlotte to revise sentence 6?

F Families think that they cannot make a difference, but this decision is wrong.

G You may not think that your family alone can make a difference, but your decisions do matter.

H Not thinking that one family can make a difference, you may not realize that your decisions matter.

J Instead of thinking that families cannot make a difference, people could realize that their decisions matter.

> **EXPLANATION:** Using a compound sentence with the coordinating conjunction *but* clearly shows a contrast between ideas. Addressing the audience with the pronoun *you* helps engage readers. The correct answer is **G.**
> - **F** is incorrect because it changes the meaning.
> - **H** and **J** are incorrect because they are awkwardly phrased and difficult for readers to understand.

TEKS 13C

GO ON ➡

3 Which transition word or phrase should Charlotte add to the beginning of sentence 9 to connect it with the ideas in sentences 6–8?

A However

B In addition

C Consequently

D In conclusion

> **EXPLANATION:** Sentence 9 provides an additional example to support the idea that a single family's appliance purchasing decisions can make a large impact. The correct answer is **B**.
> - **A** is incorrect because the ideas in sentence 9 do not differ from the rest of the paragraph.
> - **C** is incorrect because the idea in sentence 9 is not the result of a point made in the previous sentence.
> - **D** is incorrect. Sentence 9 does not summarize all of the ideas that support Charlotte's claim.

TEKS 13C

4 Charlotte wants to clarify her meaning in sentence 11. What is the most effective replacement for *by saving energy money is saved*?

F if you save energy, you save money

G to save money, save energy

H you have to save energy to save money

J when you save energy, it could save money

> **EXPLANATION:** Using the conjunction *if* simply but effectively emphasizes that saving money is a direct benefit of saving energy. The correct answer is **F**.
> - **G** and **H** are incorrect because they make unsustainable claims. Saving energy is not the only way to save money.
> - **J** is incorrect because "could save" makes the writer sound unsure of her ideas.

TEKS 13C

5 Which sentence should be deleted from this essay because it does not support or relate to Charlotte's claim?

A Sentence 14

B Sentence 15

C Sentence 16

D Sentence 17

> **EXPLANATION:** The variability in appliance prices does not relate to the counterargument that energy-efficient appliances save money in the long run. The correct answer is **A**.
> - **B, C,** and **D** are all incorrect because these sentences clearly support or relate to Charlotte's argument.

TEKS 13C

STOP

Revising Practice 1

Read the following persuasive essay. Then read each question and mark the correct answer.

Hector wrote this persuasive essay about whether teenagers should work. He would like you to read his essay and think about the improvements he should make. When you finish reading, answer the questions that follow.

Should Teenagers Work?

(1) I think it's crazy, but some people, including my mother, don't think that teenagers should work during the school year. (2) I disagree with this viewpoint. (3) Working provides teenagers with important life skills that they cannot acquire at school.

(4) By the time most teenagers are fourteen, they have already done some kind of work, such as babysitting, pet sitting, or yard maintenance. (5) Holding a regular part-time job provides opportunities to earn and to save money. (6) With a steady income, teenagers can earn enough money to help pay for their own expenses. (7) This teaches them to set financial goals and plan for the future. (8) These skills will last a lifetime.

(9) Another lesson that teenagers learn from working is responsibility. (10) Teens who work have to show up on time, be dressed appropriately, and take their jobs seriously. (11) Of course they learn these kinds of responsibilities at school, too. (12) Working teens must also learn how to communicate and develop cooperative relationships with their supervisors and coworkers. (13) Finally, working adds to teens' self-confidence.

(14) Some people argue that when teens work, they lose interest in school and their grades drop. (15) While this is a serious concern, it is not necessarily true. (16) Working can encourage teens to allocate their time wisely. (17) In fact, many teens who hold jobs do just fine in school, and there is no doubt that working shows the importance of education!

(18) When teenagers work during their high school years, they acquire responsibility and critical life skills. (19) Working helps provide teenagers with the maturity that they need in adulthood.

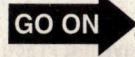
GO ON

1 How should Hector rewrite sentence 1 to focus more clearly on his topic and establish a formal tone?

A If you work during the school year, some individuals think that's a bad idea.

B My mother doesn't think that teenagers should work during the school year.

C Some individuals think that teenagers should not work during the school year.

D Working during the school year is something that some people are against.

2 Hector wants to show a contrast between the ideas in sentences 4 and 5. What is the most effective way for him to revise sentence 5?

F Once teens get a regular part-time job, they can earn and save more money.

G If you hold a regular part-time job, you could earn and save money.

H Yet to earn and to save money, they must hold a regular part-time job.

J Holding a regular part-time job, however, provides many more opportunities to earn and to save money.

3 To provide a supporting detail for his ideas, what is the most effective sentence for Hector to add after sentence 7?

A Such lessons are challenging for teens, and they must also have a lot of discipline.

B In addition, teens acquire basic skills, such as how to open and manage a bank account.

C While it is challenging for teens to control their spending, we all need to learn how to do it eventually.

D Unfortunately, some teens never learn how to set goals and plan for the future.

4 Which of the following sentences should Hector delete because it does not clearly relate to and support his claim?

F Sentence 11

G Sentence 13

H Sentence 15

J Sentence 17

5 Hector wants to use a rhetorical question in his concluding section to emphasize his claim. What is the most effective question for him to add after sentence 18?

A Isn't it true that actions speak louder than words?

B Why would anyone disagree about these issues?

C Don't you agree that working can have benefits?

D Who could deny the value of such experiences?

6 Hector wants to incorporate a metaphor in his ending sentence. What is the most effective way for him to revise sentence 19?

F Money is the spur that keeps teenagers moving on the trail ride to adulthood.

G For teenagers, a job is the sunlight and water that all living things need to grow.

H As teenagers transition to adulthood, working can help them finally see the light at the end of the tunnel.

J The maturity that teenagers develop through working becomes a helpful guide on their path through adulthood.

Name _____ Date _____

Revising Practice 2

Read the following persuasive essay. Then read each question and mark the correct answer.

Miguel wrote this persuasive essay about the issue of trash collection in his town. He would like you to read his essay and think about the improvements he should make. When you finish reading, answer the questions that follow.

Pay-As-You-Throw

(1) The town of Fairview has been struggling with its budget, and some of the strains are unnecessary. (2) The cost of trash collection is an example. (3) Rapid growth in recent years has nearly doubled the amount of waste the town must manage. (4) A pay-as-you-throw (PAYT) system for garbage collection would help alleviate the town's budget woes, promote recycling, and reduce waste.

(5) How does PAYT work? (6) The town sells special stickers or containers for this purpose. (7) Residents can purchase these items at Town Hall or at local stores. (8) For each bag or can of trash a family places on the curb, they pay a fee.

(9) When people have to pay more for creating more trash, they look for ways to cut down on waste. (10) Statistics from other towns show that PAYT has a large impact on reducing waste. (11) Since towns pay to have waste taken to a landfill or an incinerator, they save money when the waste is reduced. (12) At the same time, towns increase their revenues, because recycling companies pay them for the materials they collect.

(13) Opponents of PAYT argue that it penalizes larger households, which already pay higher taxes. (14) These larger households typically benefit more from local services, such as schools and recreation. (15) Plus, when they take full advantage of recycling and composting opportunities, larger households do not necessarily produce more trash.

(16) Other opponents of PAYT argue that Fairview's transfer station is already clogged with traffic every weekend, and that if more people try to drop off their recyclables, the situation will only get worse. (17) One way to handle this problem is to expand the hours. (18) Another solution is to start a curbside recycling program, which would allow residents to avoid the transfer station altogether. (19) Implementing either solution would still bring savings to the town with the added benefit of helping the environment.

(20) PAYT rewards people who "reduce, reuse, and recycle," instead of forcing them to subsidize their neighbors' wasteful habits. (21) The town's budget gets a boost, and we all contribute to a cleaner planet.

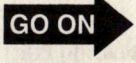

1 Miguel wants his first sentence to clearly identify the topic of his essay. What is the most effective way for him to rewrite sentences 1 and 2?

  A The cost of trash collection is an unnecessary strain on Fairview's budget, with which it has struggled.

  B The town of Fairview has been struggling with its budget, and one unnecessary strain is the cost of trash collection.

  C The cost of trash collection is an unnecessary strain on town budgets; Fairview has been struggling with its budget.

  D The town of Fairview has an unnecessary strain on its budget; the cost of trash collection is causing a struggle.

2 What is the best way for Miguel to improve the organization of sentences 5–8?

  F Switch sentences 6 and 7

  G Switch sentences 7 and 8

  H Move sentence 5 so that it follows sentence 7

  J Move sentence 8 so that it follows sentence 5

3 Miguel wants to add a supporting detail after sentence 10. What would be the most effective fact for him to add?

  A The impact of PAYT varies considerably from town to town, but it is generally always positive.

  B I have a friend whose family started recycling much more after their town started using PAYT.

  C The towns of Lexington and Milford have been successfully using PAYT programs for the past 12 years.

  D PAYT programs in Lexington and Milford have shown waste reductions of 14 and 18 percent, respectively.

4 To connect to the ideas in sentence 13, which transition word or phrase should Miguel insert at the beginning of sentence 14?

  F First

  G However

  H Therefore

  J In the meantime

5 To clarify his meaning, what is the most effective way for Miguel to revise sentence 17?

  A Expanding the hours is one way to handle this problem.

  B One way to handle this problem is to expand the hours, or make them longer.

  C One way is to expand the hours, keeping the transfer station open longer to handle this problem.

  D One way to handle this problem is to expand the hours when the transfer station is open.

6 Miguel wants to end his essay with a call to action. What would be the most effective sentence for him to add after sentence 21?

  F Ask your family if they have any ideas to alleviate the town's budget crisis.

  G Visit other towns that support PAYT and see if you notice a difference.

  H Attend the town council meeting tonight and listen to the issues discussed.

  J Contact your town council member today and urge him or her to support PAYT.

STOP

Guided Editing

Read the following essay. Then read each question and mark the correct answer.

Mim wrote this essay about the pros and cons of cell phones. She would like you to read her essay and think about the corrections she should make. When you finish reading, answer the questions that follow.

Cell Phones: The Pros and Cons

(1) They are everywhere. (2) You can't go anywhere without running into someone using one. (3) What are they? (4) Cell phones. (5) Somebody near you are always either talking or texting on a cell phone, or a weird ringtone announces a new text! (6) Of course, cell phones have many benefits. (7) They make communication so convenient that it's hard to imagine the Age when people didn't have them. (8) Cell phones also provide us with security and can save lives. (9) Kids can keep in touch with their families on the way to and from school. (10) People trapped in collapsed buildings during an earthquake or in their cars during a flood can use a cell phone to get help.

(11) However, cell phones are bad news in some ways. (12) Just because people can carry their phones with them, does that make it okay to talk loudly in public? (13) Does everyone in the vicinity have to be bombarded with one-sided conversations about the fight you had with your friend or seeing a movie? (14) Some people say, "It's a free country, so it's my right to talk in public! (15) Other people talk to their friends while they walk down the street, or eat together in a restaurant. (16) What's the difference if I talk face-to-face or on a cell?" (17) If you've been trapped in close quarters with someone having a loud cell conversation, the difference is clear.

(18) Cell phones in cars are another big problem. (19) Driving a car requires focus. (20) Whether it's a handheld or hands-free call, talking on a cell phone while driving can cause a distraction, especially if you're an inexperienced driver. (21) Texting while driving is even worse; it dangerously shifts the driver's attention from the road. (22) There have been countless accidents caused by drivers, many of them teenagers, which tried to drive and use their phones at the same time. (23) So, remember to use cell phones wisely, in and out of a car.

(24) Is there a happy medium between using a cell phone constantly or not at all? (25) Yes; it's called common sense. (26) Don't talk loudly on the phone, the person on the other end can hear just fine without your shouting. (27) Silence the phone when you're in public so you don't pollute the air that's there for all to share. (28) Finally, be respectful of the people around you, especially where safety is concerned.

GO ON

1 What change should be made in sentence 5?

A Change *are* to **is**

B Change *either* to **likewise**

C Enclose *or texting* in parentheses

D Change *announces* to **anounces**

> **EXPLANATION:** The indefinite pronoun *somebody* is singular and requires the singular verb *is*. The correct answer is **A.**
> - **B** is incorrect. The correlative conjunctions *either . . . or* correctly introduce the two possible situations of talking and texting.
> - **C** is incorrect. Parentheses should not be used because *talking* and *texting* share equal importance in the sentence.
> - **D** is incorrect. Changing the spelling of *announces* will create an error.

TEKS 13D, 17, 19

2 What change, if any, should be made in sentence 7?

F Change *Age* to **age**

G Change *make* to **made**

H Change *that* to **because**

J Make no change

> **EXPLANATION:** The names of specific historical periods should be capitalized, but this sentence makes a general reference to the time before people had cell phones. The correct answer is **F.**
> - **G** is incorrect. The present tense is correct because the sentence describes the current benefits of cell phones.
> - **H** is incorrect because it would change the meaning of the sentence.
> - **J** is incorrect. A change is necessary.

TEKS 13D, 17, 18

3 What change should be made in sentence 13?

A Change *vicinity* to **vacinity**

B Change *one-sided* to **one sided**

C Change *seeing a movie* to **the movie you saw**

D Insert a comma after *friend*

> **EXPLANATION:** Items that perform the same function in a sentence should have a parallel structure. In sentence 13, the phrase *the fight you had with your friend* is the object of the preposition *about*. To follow this structure, the second object of the preposition should be changed to begin with *the movie*. The correct answer is **C.**
> - **A** is incorrect. Changing the spelling of *vicinity* will create an error.
> - **B** is incorrect. The adjective *one-sided* requires a hyphen.
> - **D** is incorrect; the sentence is punctuated correctly.

TEKS 13D, 17, 18, 19

4 What change, if any, should be made in sentence 15?

F Change *talk* to **talked**

G Delete the comma after *street*

H Change *restaurant* to **restaraunt**

J Make no change

> **EXPLANATION:** A comma should not separate the verbs in a compound predicate. In sentence 15, there should be no comma between *walk* and *eat*. The correct answer is **G.**
> - **F** is incorrect. The present-tense form *talk* is consistent with the other verbs in the quotation, and there is no reason for a shift in tense.
> - **H** is incorrect. Changing the spelling of *restaurant* will create an error.
> - **J** is incorrect. A change is necessary.

TEKS 13D, 17, 18, 19

GO ON

5 What change should be made in sentence 22?

A Change *which* to *who*

B Delete the comma after *drivers*

C Change *their phones* to **his or her phone**

D Change *caused by drivers* to **drivers caused**

> **EXPLANATION:** The relative pronoun *which* refers to things, while *who* refers to people. In sentence 22, *who* should be used to refer to *drivers*. The correct answer is **A**.
> - **B** is incorrect. The appositive *many of them teenagers* describes the noun *drivers*. Since the phrase is not necessary to the meaning of the sentence, it should be set off by commas.
> - **C** is incorrect. Using the singular pronouns *his* and *her* to refer to the plural noun *drivers* will create an error.
> - **D** is incorrect. Placing the subject *drivers* before the verb would make the sentence unclear because *drivers* is modified by the appositive phrase and the adjective clause that immediately follow it.

TEKS 13D, 17, 18

6 What change, if any, should be made in sentence 26?

F Change *can* to *can't*

G Change *person* to *persons*

H Replace the comma with a dash

J Make no change

> **EXPLANATION:** Using a comma to join independent clauses without a conjunction creates a run-on sentence. Using a dash effectively separates the clauses and adds emphasis. The correct answer is **H**.
> - **F** is incorrect because forming a negative would change the meaning of the sentence.
> - **G** is incorrect. The singular form is correct since most phone conversations are between two people.
> - **J** is incorrect. A change is necessary.

TEKS 13D, 17B, 18

STOP

Editing Practice 1

Read the following essay. Then read each question and mark the correct answer.

Aziz wrote this essay about driving phenomenon Alice Ramsey. He would like you to read his essay and think about the corrections he should make. When you finish reading, answer the questions that follow.

Driving Sensation Alice Ramsey

(1) In the early days of the automobile, very few women drove. (2) In fact some doctors argued that simply riding in a car was unsafe for women and claimed that excessive speeds caused women to become overly excited and experience sleeping problems. (3) Alice Ramsey was the exception: she not only drove, but she loved it. (4) In 1909, she became the first woman to drive across the United States.

(5) Soon after learning to drive, Ramsey began competing in contests that tested how well drivers could handle their cars. (6) During one of these contests—a 200 mile trip to and from Montauk, New York—Ramsey caught the attention of Cadwallader Kelsey, a charismatic sales manager for the Maxwell-Brisco Car Company. (7) As a publicity stunt to generate auto sales, he challenged Ramsey to drive across the country in a Maxwell car with all expenses paid by the company. (8) Alice accepted immediately, not because she cared about car sales or publicity, but because the trip promised an adventure and a challenge she simply could not turn down.

(9) The journey began on a rainy day in New York City. (10) Ramsey brought along three female companions—two sister-in-laws and a friend—none of whom knew how to drive.

(11) Driving in those days required physical strength as well as driving skill. (12) Early automobiles were not easy to start and were subject to frequent breakdowns. (13) In addition, only 152 of the 3,600 miles the group would travel would be on paved roads. (14) Besides the rough terrain, Ramsey and her group also had to deal with torrential rains, hailstorms, and breakdowns—twelve flat tires and two broken wheel axles each, of which they had to repair themselves.

(15) Throughout the trip, enthusiastic locals waited by the roadside to cheer Ramsey. (16) Finally, fifty-nine days after Ramsey and her friends had left New York, they arrived in San Francisco to a cheering crowd. (17) Ramsey, with less than one year's driving experience, had become the first woman to drive across the country, and she had done it in a time that was less than any of the two dozen men who had made the trip before her.

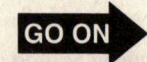

1 What change should be made in sentence 2?

A Insert a comma after *fact*

B Change *excessive* to **excesive**

C Change *claimed* to **they claimed**

D Change *overly excited* to **over excited**

2 What change should be made in sentence 6?

F Change *200 mile* to **200-mile**

G Delete the comma after *Montauk*

H Change *charismatic* to **charasmatic**

J Change *sales manager* to **Sales Manager**

3 What change, if any, should be made in sentence 8?

A Change *could not* to **did not**

B Change *accepted* to **had accepted**

C Replace the comma after *publicity* with a colon

D Make no change

4 What change should be made in sentence 10?

F Change *whom* to **which**

G Change *knew* to **knowing**

H Change the dashes to commas

J Change *sister-in-laws* to **sisters-in-law**

5 What change should be made in sentence 14?

A Insert a colon after *with*

B Change *torrential* to **torential**

C Replace *axles each, of* with **axles, each of**

D Change *themselves* to **itself**

6 What change, if any, should be made in sentence 17?

F Change *year's* to **years**

G Change *experience* to **experiences**

H Change *in a time that was less* to **in less time**

J Make no change

Editing Practice 2

Amelia wrote this essay about the Special Olympics. She would like you to read her essay and think about the corrections she should make. When you finish reading, answer the questions that follow.

The Special Olympics

(1) Every two years, Americans across the country cheer for our nation's best athletes as they compete in the Olympic Games. (2) In the summer, we watch gymnasts, swimmers, and track stars accomplish amazing feats. (3) Then, in the winter, we watch as skiers take incredible risks and ice skaters flew, float, and jump across the ice. (4) There is another olympics, however, whose games get less attention. (5) The Special Olympics honor the efforts and achievements of intellectually disabled athletes. (6) My parents and I became volunteers for this organization several years ago. (7) My younger sister, who was born with Down syndrome, has become a swimmer in the Special Olympics. (8) It is a lot of work for my sister to train for these games. (9) Nonetheless, she trains constantly, swimming every day working diligently with her coach. (10) My sister truly lives out the Special Olympics oath: "Let me win. But if I cannot win, let me be brave in the attempt."

(11) The history of the Special Olympics began with a very special woman, Eunice Kennedy Shriver. (12) Mrs. Shriver knew that people with mental disabilities could enjoy the benefits of physical activity. (13) In 1962, they started a summer camp, and young people with disabilities came to her home to swim, run, and play soccer. (14) Summer camp programs for the disabled were then started in parks around the country. (15) In 1968, the First International Special Olympic Games were organized and held in Chicago, Illinois. (16) One thousand athletes participated. (17) At the 1995 World Games, 7,000 athletes competed, and today the program serves more than 2.5 million children and adults in over 180 countries. (18) Mrs. Shriver died in 2009, but her legacy through these wonderful games for people with disabilities.

(19) The mission of the Special Olympics is to provide year round sports training and athletic competition in a variety of sports for children and adults with intellectual disabilities. (20) Participants experience athletic achievement, gain confidence, and make new friends. (21) For my sister and many others, this mission has indeed been accomplished.

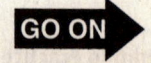

1 What change should be made in
sentence 3?

- **A** Change *flew* to **fly**
- **B** Change *take* to **took**
- **C** Change *and jump* to **and they jump**
- **D** Change *watch* to **watched**

2 What change, if any, should be made in
sentence 4?

- **F** Change *get* to **gets**
- **G** Change *olympics* to **Olympics**
- **H** Delete the comma after *olympics*
- **J** Make no change

3 What change should be made in
sentence 9?

- **A** Change *diligently* to **dillegently**
- **B** Change *working* to **and working**
- **C** Change *Nonetheless* to **None-the-less**
- **D** Replace the comma after *constantly*
  with a semicolon

4 What change, if any, should be made in
sentence 13?

- **F** Change *they* to **she**
- **G** Change *disabilities* to **a disability**
- **H** Insert a dash between *home* and *to*
- **J** Make no change

5 What change should be made in
sentence 18?

- **A** Change *for* to **found**
- **B** Change *but* to **following**
- **C** Change *died* to **had died**
- **D** Insert **lives on** after *legacy*

6 What change, if any, should be made in
sentence 19?

- **F** Insert a comma after *is*
- **G** Change *intellectual* to **intelectual**
- **H** Change *year round* to **year-round**
- **J** Make no change

STOP

Part II

Texas Write Source
Assessments

Pretest

Part 1: Improving Sentences and Paragraphs

> **Questions 1–6: Read each sentence. Choose the best way to write the underlined part of the sentence. Fill in the circle of the correct answer on your answer document.**

1 Along with Ben Jonson and Christopher Marlowe, William Shakespeare <u>were</u> one of three great Elizabethan playwrights.

  A are

  B was

  C being

  D Make no change

2 <u>The son of John Shakespeare, a butcher, William Shakespeare was born in 1564 in Stratford-on-Avon.</u>

  F William Shakespeare, the son of a butcher named John Shakespeare, was born in Stratford-on-Avon in 1564.

  G William Shakespeare was born the son of John Shakespeare in 1564, a butcher, in Stratford-on-Avon.

  H William Shakespeare was born the son of a Stratford-on-Avon butcher, John Shakespeare, in 1564.

  J Make no change

3 Shakespeare's early life, <u>about whom very little is known,</u> may have included some time served as a soldier before he went on stage as an actor.

  A about whatever very little is known,

  B about which very little is known,

  C about what very little is known,

  D Make no change

4 Although he is credited with more than 35 dramas, some people believe that a mere butcher's son and actor <u>couldn't write all those plays.</u>

  F couldn't of written all those plays.

  G couldn't be writing all those plays.

  H couldn't have written all those plays.

  J Make no change

GO ON →

5 Christopher Marlowe, born the same year as Shakespeare, was a popular figure <u>who lived glamorous and died youthfully</u> in a tavern brawl.

A who lived glamorously and died at a young age

B who lived in a glamorous manner and died youngly

C who lived glamorous and died young

D Make no change

6 <u>For Ben Jonson, his first play was called</u> *Every Man in His Humor*, <u>that was</u> <u>performed</u> at the Curtain Theatre in 1598 with Shakespeare in the cast.

F Ben Jonson, whose first play was called *Every Man in His Humor*, which was performed

G For Ben Jonson, his first play that was performed was called *Every Man in His Humor*

H Ben Jonson's first play, *Every Man in His Humor*, was performed

J Make no change

Questions 7–8: Read each question and fill in the circle of the correct answer on your answer document.

---

7 Which is a complete sentence written correctly?

A The men who murdered Marlowe in 1593 were probably hired by Queen Elizabeth's spymaster, Lord Walsingham, did not trust Marlowe, who was a spy as well as a playwright.

B Many of the plays written in the late sixteenth and early seventeenth centuries are tragedies of bloody revenge, to which Shakespeare's *Hamlet* belongs.

C In Shakespeare's time, plays were often the work of teams or pairs of writers, of whom Shakespeare collaborated with John Fletcher on *The Two Noble Kinsmen.*

D The original Globe Theatre burned down in 1613 after a special effect involving a cannon went disastrously wrong during a performance of *Henry VIII.*

8 Which is the best way to combine these two sentences?

> The young Shakespeare was an accomplished actor by the age of 28. Shakespeare helped to establish the Globe Theatre in 1599.

F The young Shakespeare, who helped establish the Globe Theatre at age 28, became an accomplished actor in 1599.

G Shakespeare, an accomplished young actor, helped to establish the Globe Theatre in 1599 at the age of 28.

H The young Shakespeare was an accomplished actor by the age of 28, he helped to establish the Globe Theatre in 1599.

J Shakespeare, an accomplished actor by the age of 28, helped to establish the Globe Theatre in 1599.

GO ON

Questions 9–14 refer to the following passage. Read the passage. Then read each question. Fill in the circle of the correct answer on your answer document.

(1) The Greek philosopher Socrates was born around 470 B.C. and died in 399 B.C. (2) Although none of Socrates' writings exist, we know about his theories and methods through his pupil Plato (427 B.C.–348 B.C.). (3) Plato's philosophical works were written in the form of dramatic dialogues. (4) Socrates appears as the principal figure in these dialogues. (5) Many of these dialogues survive, but some may not be genuine.

(6) As a philosopher, Socrates was mainly concerned with ethics, which is the branch of philosophy that considers questions of right and wrong. (7) The foundation of Socrates' ethics was the belief that virtue is knowledge and that all human wickedness is the result of ignorance. (8) He aimed to demonstrate that the answers to the most profound ethical questions lie in the minds of all people. (9) Socrates sought to find the truth by asking simple but searching questions. (10) Most people, according to Socrates, lead what he called "unexamined lives," and his aim was to enable people to examine themselves and thus discover the truth.

(11) His method was to present himself as an ignorant man who needed to be told the simplest and most basic things. (12) Typically, Socrates would ask one of his students a question, and when he answered, Socrates would ask innocently: "Why do you think this is so?" (13) More seemingly innocent questions would follow, each one harder to answer than the last. (14) This technique, known as the "Socratic method," was one of the philosopher's most important legacies. (15) The wise philosopher's pretended ignorance in the pursuit of knowledge is called "Socratic irony."

9 Which sentence is not relevant to the writer's argument and should be removed?

A Plato's philosophical works were written in the form of dramatic dialogues.

B Many of these dialogues survive, but some may not be genuine.

C Socrates sought to find the truth by asking simple but searching questions.

D His method was to present himself as an ignorant man who needed to be told the simplest and most basic things.

10 Which is the best way to join the two underlined sentences (3 and 4) to make a single sentence?

F Plato's philosophical works were written in the form of dramatic dialogues, for Socrates appears as the principal figure in these dialogues.

G Plato's philosophical works were written in the form of dramatic dialogues, because in them Socrates appears as the principal figure.

H Plato's philosophical works are written in the form of dramatic dialogues, in which Socrates appears as the principal figure.

J Although Plato's philosophical works were written in the form of dramatic dialogues, Socrates appears in them as the principal figure.

GO ON

11 Which sentence from the passage is a complex sentence?

A sentence 2

B sentence 5

C sentence 9

D sentence 15

12 Which would be the best clause or phrase to insert into sentence 8 to link it to sentences 9 and 10?

F Like a master detective,

G As a teacher,

H Though he was undeterred by all evidence to the contrary,

J Like a modern-day physician,

13 Which of these would be the best sentence to insert before sentence 11 to introduce the third paragraph?

A Unfortunately, Socrates often came across as a ridiculous figure in Plato's dialogues.

B Socrates' persistent questioning was probably as irritating to his pupils as it is to modern-day readers.

C Socrates was like a philosophical dog with a bone.

D In each dialogue, Socrates forced his students to analyze their thoughts and feelings.

14 Which sentence should be added after sentence 15 to conclude this piece?

F In a different form of irony, though, Socrates the teacher was later sentenced to death for corrupting the minds of young Athenians.

G Of course, Socrates' pupils played along with his tricks because they wanted to find out the truth, too.

H As we see, philosophy can be fun!

J Of course, Socrates was certainly not ignorant, no matter how much he pretended to be.

Questions 15–20: A student wrote this passage. It may need some changes or corrections. Read the passage. Then read each question. Fill in the circle of the correct answer on your answer document.

---

(1) Have you ever noticed that very few children's adventure stories take place at home? (2) Typically, the hero or heroine leaves or is removed from home so that the adventure may develop without watchful parents and the need to go to school. (3) *The Chronicles of Narnia* and *Peter Pan* come to mind as examples of these tales. (4) The hero or heroine often goes to stay with relatives—ideally, grandparents or an elderly aunt—who will be kind, trusting, and indulgent. (5) These relations should be as elderly as possible so that they will be able to offer sage advice when needed but will be unable to restrain the child from having the adventure. (6) They may own a dog or a cat but rarely a parakeet or goldfish. (7) In some versions of the set-up for an adventure story, the child will be recovering from an illness and in need of fresh air and exercise.

(8) The fresh air and exercise the main character needs will be found in the mountains or by the ocean. (9) Both locations offer many story possibilities. (10) Mountains in children's fiction are often swarming with wild animals and eccentric hermits. (11) Often the child will win the trust of a bear or wolf and learn the ways of the wild from some cranky mountain-dweller. (12) By the ocean, there are bold seafarers to befriend, rocky coves to explore, and boats to take the hero or heroine to a mysterious island. (13) There may also be strange creatures and spooky houses, but these are less frequent nowadays because modern children generally are not encouraged to believe in the such things. (14) Storytellers in Victorian times, on the other hand, often used strange effects and creatures to frighten their readers.

15 What type of passage is this?

A personal narrative
B comparison-contrast essay
C persuasive essay
D informative article

16 What pattern of organization does the writer use to organize these two paragraphs?

F chronological order
G comparison and contrast
H thesis with supporting examples
J problem and solution

17 Which would be the best clause or phrase to insert at the beginning of sentence 8 to help make the transition to the ideas in the next paragraph?

    A In many of these stories,

    B In my opinion,

    C It is a well-established fact that

    D In the kind of stories you read,

18 Which sentence is inappropriate and should be removed from this passage?

    F The hero or heroine goes to stay with relatives—ideally grandparents or an elderly aunt—who will be kind, trusting, and indulgent.

    G They may own a dog or a cat but rarely a parakeet or goldfish.

    H In some versions of the set-up for an adventure story, the child will be recovering from an illness and in need of fresh air and exercise.

    J Often the child will win the trust of a bear or wolf and learn the ways of the wild from some cranky mountain-dweller.

19 Which sentence could best be inserted before sentence 8 to add to readers' understanding?

    A Where would you go to recover from an illness?

    B The convalescent child is a favorite character in children's fiction.

    C Kids who are sick play a big part in lots of stories.

    D Encounters with wild animals and mysterious strangers are important.

20 If this passage continued, what information would be most logical to add in the next paragraph of the passage?

    F further comparisons between Victorian and modern-day children's fiction

    G some examples of adventures that can take place at home

    H some remarks about the kinds of children's stories the writer enjoys

    J concluding remarks about how the lessons learned from such adventures can be applied to everyday life

GO ON

Part 2: Correcting Sentence Errors

Questions 21–26: Read each sentence. One of the underlined parts may be an error in grammar or usage. Decide which underlined part, if any, should be corrected. Fill in the circle of the correct answer on your answer document.

21 My mother <u>has probably seen</u>
              A

<u>"Gone with the Wind"</u> twenty times, and
    B

<u>every time she sees it,</u> <u>she says the same</u>
       C   **D**

<u>thing</u>: "I could watch that movie every day of

my life and not get tired of it!"

<u>Make no change.</u>
    E

22 <u>Although my opinion</u> <u>may not carry</u> as much
     F   **G**

weight as <u>yours or hers,</u> I'm just as entitled
         H

to speak my mind <u>as you are or she is.</u>
             J

<u>Make no change.</u>
    K

23 <u>Sarah's</u> <u>cat's</u> curiosity is more worrying than
    A   **B**

ever, now that <u>he's started climbing</u>
             C

into <u>other peoples' sheds and cabins.</u>
      D

<u>Make no change.</u>
    E

24 After Dan <u>had mowed the lawn</u> and
             F

<u>taken the dog for a walk,</u>
        G

he <u>barely had no time left</u> to eat his
       H

breakfast <u>before going to school.</u>
        J

<u>Make no change.</u>
    K

25 It was unfair <u>to criticize</u> anyone,
         A

since <u>nobody</u> could have
     B

<u>completed the work efficiently</u> in <u>the time</u>
       C   **D**

alotted. <u>Make no change.</u>
     E

26 The room was <u>completely silent</u> as the
         F

hooded figure <u>slipped in through the</u>
            G

<u>window,</u> <u>Even the furniture</u> seemed to be
        H

<u>holding its breath.</u> <u>Make no change.</u>
    J   **K**

Questions 27–32: Read the passage. Choose the best way to write each underlined part. Fill in the circle of the correct answer on your answer document.

The ancient Romans thought that a person should have "a healthy mind in

a <u>healthy body", and</u> they were right. We would all like to be able to go through
      27

life in a state of excellent physical fitness and sanity. However, <u>its probably</u>
                                                   28

much harder these days to stay healthy in mind and body than it was in Julius

Caesar's time. In <u>Ancient Rome</u>, people weren't tempted by fast food. They
              29

didn't watch TV all day and night. They didn't have automobiles <u>either—if they</u>
                                                   30

wanted to get somewhere, they usually had to walk. These days we have so

many opportunities to become unhealthy and overweight, it's amazing that

anyone can still walk at all. It's also a miracle that anyone's able to think

rationally, <u>bombarded as we be</u> with words and images designed to manipulate
              31

our thoughts and mold our judgment. It is an <u>allusion</u> to think that any Roman
                                                 32

soldier could march forty miles and stay sane after a month of American TV

and a diet of take-out pizza!

27 A healthy body." And
  B healthy body" and
  C healthy body," and
  D Make no change

28 F its' probably
  G it's probably
  H it probably is
  J Make no change

29 A ancient Rome
  B ancient rome
  C Ancient rome
  D Make no change

30 F either . . . if they
  G either, if they
  H either: if they
  J Make no change

31 A bombarded as we would be
  B bombarded as we are
  C bombarded as we were
  D Make no change

32 F assent
  G illusion
  H effect
  J Make no change

GO ON

Part 3: Writing   Expository

READ

Many Americans enjoy watching sports, such as baseball, football, basketball, and hockey. To watch college or professional sports, you can buy a ticket and see the game live at the ballpark, stadium, or arena. In many cases, you also have the option of staying home and watching the game on television.

THINK

Think about the differences between watching a sporting event live and watching it on TV. What are the advantages and disadvantages of each experience?

WRITE

Write an essay in which you briefly compare and contrast the experiences of watching a sporting event live and viewing it on television.

As you write your composition, remember to —

☐ include a thesis statement that introduces the comparison and contrast between watching sports live and on TV

☐ organize your ideas in a logical order, and connect those ideas using transitions

☐ develop your ideas fully and thoughtfully with well-chosen details and observations

☐ make sure your composition is no longer than one page

Progress Test 1

Part 1: Improving Sentences and Paragraphs

> **Questions 1–6: Read each sentence. Choose the best way to write the underlined part of the sentence. Fill in the circle of the correct answer on your answer document.**

1 Louis Armstrong once said that if you had to ask <u>what jazz are</u>, you would never know.

   A what jazz were
   B what jazz was
   C what jazz had been
   D Make no change

2 Jazz is derived primarily from a simple musical form known as the blues, <u>which have</u> musical and cultural roots stretching back to West Africa.

   F which has
   G that have
   H which having
   J Make no change

3 The earliest jazz evolved in New Orleans from the processional brass band and popular dance music of that <u>vibrantly multicultural</u> city.

   A vibrant multicultural
   B vibrant multiculturally
   C vibrantly multiculturally
   D Make no change

4 Buddy Bolden and his band took a giant step forward <u>when he developed</u> the style of group improvisation that we associate with classic New Orleans jazz.

   F when they developed
   G when it developed
   H when this developed
   J Make no change

GO ON ➡

5 The greatest saxophonists in the history of jazz are Charlie Parker and John Coltrane, <u>however</u> some would claim that the greatest of all is Sidney Bechet.

   A nevertheless

   B although

   C meanwhile

   D Make no change

6 Thelonious Monk, a jazz pianist of many talents, <u>were</u> one of the musicians who developed "bebop" in the 1940s.

   F are

   G being

   H was

   J Make no change

Questions 7–8: Read each question and fill in the circle of the correct answer on your answer document.

---

7 Which is a run-on sentence that should be written as two sentences?

   A Igor Stravinsky, the great Russian composer, believed that jazz was America's greatest contribution to twentieth century music.

   B Lester Young, who played tenor saxophone and often accompanied singer Billie Holiday, his nickname was "Pres," which was short for "President."

   C Sidney Bechet, who was born in New Orleans, moved to Paris in 1950 to get away from the racial prejudice he encountered in the United States.

   D Edward Kennedy "Duke" Ellington, one of many jazz musicians whose nicknames came from British aristocracy, began his career as a pianist in small dance bands.

8 Which is an interrogative sentence that should end with a question mark?

   F I wonder why Charlie Parker was nicknamed "Bird"

   G Miles Davis was sometimes asked why he wore such extraordinary clothes

   H "What is jazz?" is a question that Louis Armstrong found impossible to answer

   J If jazz is this country's greatest contribution to music, what is its second greatest

GO ON ➡

Questions 9–14 refer to the following passage. Read the passage. Then read each question. Fill in the circle of the correct answer on your answer document.

(1) There are many ways to read Herman Melville's novel *Moby-Dick*. (2) First, it is a great adventure story. (3) It is the tale of a whaler's long, perilous quest to find and kill Moby-Dick. (4) The great white whale is the greatest prize of all. (5) The story is intensely dramatic, packed with action, and told in a narrative voice that is as authentic as tarred twine. (6) Epic in scale and filled with larger-than-life characters, *Moby-Dick* is the greatest tale of high adventure ever written by an American author.

(7) On a second level, *Moby-Dick* is an informational book about whaling. (8) Only about half the text is directly concerned with the story itself. (9) The rest of the book is taken up with a series of long, nonfiction passages on whales and whaling, navigation, American history, religion, mythology, science, and even on the nature of whiteness. (10) It has been said that after reading *Moby-Dick,* you could rig and prepare a whaling vessel, recruit a good crew, and take to the ocean.

(11) The third level on which *Moby-Dick* operates is more mysterious. (12) It can be read as an allegory, which means there is a symbolic structure of meaning that underlies the literal narrative. (13) The names of the characters give clues. (14) Captain Ahab is named for a king from the Bible who was ruined by love for his unfaithful wife, Jezebel. (15) Ishmael, the crewman who survives to tell the tale, is named for the outcast son of the biblical Abraham. (16) His name not only stands for all outcasts but refers to a person who tells a story. (17) Some of the crewmen's names, like Flask and Stubb, hint at hidden meanings under the dark surface of the story. (18) Also lurking under the surface, there is the great white whale itself.

9 What kind of passage is this?

  A informational article
  B personal narrative
  C interpretive response to literature
  D persuasive essay

10 What pattern of organization did the writer use in this passage?

  F comparison and contrast
  G order of importance
  H classification order
  J problem and solution

GO ON →

11 What is the best way to combine underlined sentences 3 and 4?

A It is the tale of a whaler's long, perilous quest to find and kill the greatest prize of all: Moby-Dick, the great white whale.

B It is the tale of a whaler's long, perilous quest to find and kill Moby-Dick, the great white whale, the greatest prize of all.

C It is the tale of a long, perilous quest to find Moby-Dick, the great white whale that is the greatest prize of all, and kill it.

D It is the tale of a whaler's long, perilous quest to find the great white whale, and kill Moby-Dick, the greatest prize of all.

12 In the second paragraph, which is the topic sentence?

F On a second level, *Moby-Dick* is an informational book about whaling.

G Only about half the text is directly concerned with the story itself.

H The rest of the book is taken up with a series of long, nonfiction passages on whales and whaling, navigation, American history, religion, mythology, science, and even on the nature of whiteness.

J It has been said that after reading *Moby-Dick,* you could rig and prepare a whaling vessel, recruit a good crew, and take to the ocean.

13 Which sentence could be added after sentence 5 to provide useful detail?

A Melville was sometimes amused by how sailors talked.

B Melville had been to sea and knew some things about whales and other stuff.

C Twine, or heavy thread, was often tarred aboard ship to make it waterproof.

D Melville was an experienced sailor, with a vast store of knowledge from the several voyages he made as a young man.

14 Which sentence should be added after sentence 18 to conclude this piece?

F What's *that* all about?

G What Moby-Dick really is, is anybody's guess.

H This powerful symbol seems to mean something different to everyone who reads the book.

J Scientists cannot confirm that any white whale of Moby-Dick's size has ever existed, nor can they explain how a whale would be all white.

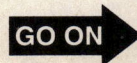
GO ON

Questions 15–20: A student wrote this passage. It may need some changes or corrections. Read the passage. Then read each question. Fill in the circle of the correct answer on your answer document.

(1) I fully believe that in years to come, historians will look back and say that the most important invention of our age was the Internet. (2) Just as Gutenberg's invention of movable type in the fifteenth century revolutionized the written word and Lenoir's invention of the internal combustion engine revolutionized transport, so the invention of the Internet has revolutionized the way we communicate, the way we use information, and even the way we think.

(3) Some people claim that the cell phone is more important, since it allows us to communicate wherever we are. (4) Others say the personal computer is more important, the Internet is just one out of many important functions of computer technology. (5) However, I would say to them that the cell phone is just a development of existing technology, and the personal computer will be seen in time merely as a tool for accessing the Internet. (6) I also happen to think cell phones are barbaric. (7) The sheer size and scope of the Internet boggles the mind—and it grows more mind-boggling with every second that passes. (8) This vast treasure trove is open to the world at the click of a mouse—and it's as free as the air!

15 What kind of passage is this?

A editorial

B expository article

C personal narrative

D argumentative essay

16 Which sentence is inappropriate and should be removed from this passage?

F I fully believe that in years to come, historians will look back and say that the most important invention of our age was the Internet.

G Just as Gutenberg's invention of movable type in the fifteenth century revolutionized the written word, and Lenoir's invention of the internal combustion engine revolutionized transport, so the invention of the Internet has revolutionized the way we communicate, the way we use information, and even the way we think.

H I also happen to think cell phones are barbaric.

J This vast treasure trove is open to the world at the click of a mouse—and it's as free as the air!

GO ON

17 Which would be the best sentence to insert after sentence 1 to link it to sentence 2?

   A I believe it is right up there with some other great inventions.

   B We live in an age of important inventions, but none has had the impact that the Internet has had.

   C It could in fact prove to be the greatest invention since the wheel.

   D Nobody can even describe what the Internet is like or the changes it has brought about.

18 Which is a run-on sentence that should be written as two sentences?

   F Just as Gutenberg's invention of movable type in the fifteenth century revolutionized the written word and Lenoir's invention of the internal combustion engine revolutionized transport, so the invention of the Internet has revolutionized the way we communicate, the way we use information, and even the way we think.

   G Others say the personal computer is more important, the Internet is just one out of many important functions of computer technology.

   H The sheer size and scope of the Internet boggles the mind—and it grows more mind-boggling with every second that passes.

   J This vast treasure trove is open to the world at the click of a mouse—and it's as free as the air!

19 Which is the best way to rewrite sentences 7 and 8 to conclude the passage?

   A The Internet is the greatest store of information ever generated, and it's growing bigger every second. It's accessible to everyone who has a computer—and it's free!

   B The Internet is unimaginably vast, and it's becoming even more unimaginably greater with every second that passes. It's open to the world—and it doesn't cost a cent to explore it!

   C The Internet is big, and it's growing bigger every second. Everyone who has a computer can access it, and it's also free too.

   D The Internet is a universe unto itself, and that universe expands with every second that ticks by. All you need to access this exploding cosmos is a computer—and there's no entry fee either!

20 Which detail sentence could best be inserted after sentence 2 to add to the readers' understanding?

   F Internet communication is faster than thought itself, and no human memory can compete with the Internet's endless resource of instantly accessible facts.

   G It's only a matter of time before the Internet will be able to communicate thought itself, and as a resource of facts it is already more reliable than human memory.

   H The Internet thinks faster, talks faster, and remembers more than we do.

   J E-mail and Internet messaging are instant, and the Internet has already evolved into a resource of information more rapidly and reliably accessible than the human memory.

GO ON →

Part 2: Correcting Sentence Errors

> Questions 21–26: Read each sentence. One of the underlined parts may be an error in grammar or usage. Decide which underlined part, if any, should be corrected. Fill in the circle of the correct answer on your answer document.

21 My grandmother <u>always insisted</u> that
A

<u>whomever came to visit</u>, <u>whether it was</u> the
B   C

next-door neighbor or the President of the

United States, <u>had to leave</u> his shoes at the
D

doorstep. <u>Make no change.</u>
E

22 As he stood <u>facing the opposition</u> with his
F

teammates <u>and heard the roar</u> of the huge
G

crowd, <u>George felt more nervous</u> and
H

excited <u>than him had ever felt in his life</u>.
J

<u>Make no change.</u>
K

23 The <u>only site</u> Morrison could see as he
A

<u>gazed across</u> the <u>flat, dusty</u> surface of the
B   C

planet was the <u>weather tower</u> he and his
D

crewmates had erected. <u>Make no change.</u>
E

24 <u>"Falling asleep</u> during the concert was
F

<u>unforgivable,"</u> the conductor told the red-
G

faced <u>clarinetist</u>, <u>"and if you had come</u>
H   J

straight back to the hotel last night instead

of going to the movies, it wouldn't have

happened." <u>Make no change.</u>
K

25 <u>The chilled shrimp</u> and the roast lamb were
A

both very good <u>(the lamb was particularly</u>
B

<u>succulent)</u>, but the *pommes* frites tasted like
C

<u>soggy sponges.</u> <u>Make no change.</u>
D   E

26 When we asked <u>if we were going to be</u>
F

punished for <u>taking a midnight swim</u> in the
G

lake, our counselor said <u>this wasn't neither</u>
H

<u>the time nor the place</u> to discuss <u>the issue</u>.
J

<u>Make no change.</u>
K

GO ON ➡

> **Questions 27–32: Read the passage. Choose the best way to write each underlined part. Fill in the circle of the correct answer on your answer document.**

Dear Ms. Wheeler:

I happened to be walking past your store last night and saw the advertisement in the window for a part-time sales assistant. I called earlier today and was advised by one of your very unhelpful staff to write a letter of application to you personally. I think I may be just the person <u>your</u> looking for!
27

I am 17 years old, and I am just finishing eleventh grade at the Cab Calloway High School for the Performing Arts. Summer vacation begins on June 10th. I have to tell you that yours are not the kind of clothes I usually wear, but I'd probably be a good model for them as I am <u>6´ 2˝ and weigh only</u>
28
<u>110 lbs</u>. I should also warn you that I'm <u>allergick</u> to all artificial fibers.
29

If I get this job, can I occasionally take time off to rehearse with my <u>band.</u> When we play a gig, I won't be available for work until noon the next
30
day at the earliest. I should also tell you that I am unable to do any heavy lifting as I am a dancer, not a <u>Manual Laborer</u>.
31

As a rule, I do not give out my cell phone number to <u>strangers—but</u>
32
you can call my mom (555-1234), and she'll forward any messages.

Yours sincerely,

Buffy Van Blythe

27 **A** youre

B you're

C your'e

D Make no change

30 **F** band?

G band!

H band;

J Make no change

28 **F** 6 foot 2 ins and weigh only 110 lbs

G Six two and weigh only 110 lbs

H 6 ft 2 ins and weigh only 110 pounds

J Make no change

31 **A** Manual laborer

B manual Laborer

C manual laborer

D Make no change

29 **A** allergict

B alergic

C allergic

D Make no change

32 **F** strangers; but

G strangers . . . but

H strangers: but

J Make no change

Part 3: Writing   Narrative

READ

We've all experienced the feeling that we have been somewhere, seen something, met someone, or done something before, when in fact we know perfectly well that we haven't. This feeling is called *déjà vu*—a French phrase that means "already seen."

THINK

Think about a time when you had that strange feeling of having been somewhere or seen something before. What details can you remember? How did you react?

WRITE

Write a personal narrative describing a time when you experienced *déjà vu*.

As you write your composition, remember to —

☐ write a thoughtful and engaging narrative, making use of literary techniques and devices such as dialogue and suspense

☐ develop one central conflict through its climax and resolution

☐ recount events in an order that makes sense, and make that order clear to readers

☐ make sure your composition is no longer than one page

Progress Test 2

Part 1: Improving Sentences and Paragraphs

Questions 1–6: Read each sentence. Choose the best way to write the underlined part of the sentence. Fill in the circle of the correct answer on your answer document.

1 On April 15, 1874, an exhibition of work by a group of young artists <u>who's</u> paintings had been rejected by the French Academy of Fine Arts opened at a studio in Paris.

A whose
B which
C for whom
D Make no change

2 Among the paintings in the exhibition <u>were</u> Claude Monet's *Impression, Sunrise,* a large oil painting of Le Havre harbor at dawn.

F being
G are
H was
J Make no change

3 Monet's picture was ridiculed <u>by</u> art critic Louis Leroy, who remarked that, in spite of the title, the painting did not make much of an impression.

A for
B about
C of
D Make no change

4 The group of painters we know as the "Impressionists" <u>include</u> Claude Monet, Edouard Manet, and Auguste Renoir.

F including
G includes
H are including
J Make no change

GO ON

5 Thirty-one artists took part in the 1874 exhibition, but the number <u>shrunk</u> in subsequent years because the organizers bickered constantly over who were Impressionists and who were not.

A was shrunk
B shrinked
C shrank
D Make no change

6 Impressionists used paint in a different way from previous artists, <u>laying it on thick</u> and creating rich textures by applying wet paint quickly over layers of paint that were not yet dry.

F laying it on thickly
G laying it on in a thick way
H laying it on more thick
J Make no change

Questions 7–8: Read each question and fill in the circle of the correct answer on your answer document.

---

7 What is the best way to combine these two sentences?

> Paul Cézanne was a contributor to the 1874 exhibition and was one of the original Impressionists.
> Paul Cézanne later became associated with the Post-Impressionists, such as van Gogh and Gauguin.

A As a contributor to the 1874 exhibition, Paul Cézanne was one of the original Impressionists; but he later became associated with the Post-Impressionists, such as van Gogh and Gauguin.

B Paul Cézanne contributed to the 1874 exhibition and was one of the original Impressionists; also, he later became associated with the Post-Impressionists, such as van Gogh and Gauguin.

C Paul Cézanne was one of the original Impressionists since he contributed to the 1874 exhibition, so he later became associated with the Post-Impressionists, such as van Gogh and Gauguin.

D Since Paul Cézanne was one of the original Impressionists and contributed to the 1874 exhibition, he later became associated with the Post-Impressionists, such as van Gogh and Gauguin.

8 What is the best way to improve this sentence to make it more interesting?

> Vincent van Gogh died penniless in 1890.

F Vincent van Gogh was a painter who died in 1890, and he was penniless when he died.

G While Vincent van Gogh died without a penny to his name, he was also a painter who died in 1890.

H Vincent van Gogh was a painter, he was penniless, and he died in 1890.

J Although Dutch artist Vincent van Gogh died penniless in 1890, today his paintings are worth millions.

GO ON

Questions 9–14 refer to the following passage. Read the passage. Then read each question. Fill in the circle of the correct answer on your answer document.

(1) Edson Arantes do Nascimento, nicknamed Pelé, was born on October 23, 1940. (2) Soccer was in his blood—his father, João Ramos "Dondinho" do Nascimento played for the Brazilian first division club Fluminese. (3) When Edson was born, his father touched the baby's legs and said, "One day, he will be a great footballer." (4) Brazilian athletes earned very little money, and Edson learned to play soccer by kicking a paper-stuffed sock out on the streets of Bauru in eastern Brazil. (5) When he was nine years old, a school friend gave him his nickname, Pelé.

(6) At the age of fifteen, Pelé joined Santos, a professional team in the city of São Paulo. (7) Only ten months after his professional debut, he was called up to the Brazilian national team. (8) In 1958, at the age of seventeen, he scored two goals in the World Cup against Sweden. (9) Pelé was to play in three more World Cups, and by the time he retired from international soccer in 1974, he had become a legend throughout the world.

(10) Pelé was the most complete player in the history of soccer. (11) He was extremely fast, and when he dribbled the ball, it seemed to be attached invisibly to his boots with elastic. (12) His feinting and tackling left defenders baffled and falling in his wake. (13) His silky samba rhythms turned every game into a carnival. (14) His shooting was lethal from any angle and any distance. (15) Perhaps his most famous shot is the "bicycle kick," which involved turning a back somersault in the air and kicking the ball over his head. (16) Since his retirement, Pelé has been Brazilian Sports Minister, United Nations Ambassador for Ecology and Environment, and an Ambassador for UNESCO.

9 Which is the best sentence to insert before sentence 1 to make the introductory paragraph more appealing to readers?

A Of all the great soccer players that Brazil has produced, Pelé is probably the greatest of all.

B It is said that soccer is a religion in Brazil, and if that is so, its deity is the subject of this essay.

C Brazil has produced more great soccer players than any other nation in the world, although Argentina was the birthplace of one of the all-time greats.

D Who is the greatest soccer player of them all?

10 Which detail sentence could best be added after sentence 10?

F He was also very good-natured.

G He had more skills than three other players put together.

H Some say that Franz Beckenbauer of West Germany was the best all-round player.

J It is unlikely that there will ever be a player to match Pelé.

GO ON

11 What word or phrase should be added to the beginning of sentence 4 to link it with sentence 3?

    A In those days,
    B Unfortunately,
    C Nevertheless,
    D As a result,

12 Which is the best sentence to insert before sentence 6 to introduce the ideas in the second paragraph?

    F The youngster truly loved to play the game.
    G The young man's extraordinary talents were quickly recognized.
    H Dondinho's prophecy eventually came true.
    J Golden opportunities came knocking on the young man's door.

13 Which sentence is inappropriate and should be removed from the passage?

    A When Edson was born, his father touched the baby's legs and said, "One day, he will be a great footballer."
    B At the age of fifteen, Pelé joined Santos, a professional team in the city of São Paulo.
    C His silky samba rhythms turned every game into a carnival.
    D Since his retirement, Pelé has been Brazilian Sports Minister, UN Ambassador for Ecology and Environment, and an Ambassador for UNESCO.

14 What pattern of organization did the writer use in this passage?

    F comparison and contrast
    G classification order
    H order of location
    J chronological order

GO ON

Questions 15–20: A student wrote this passage. It may need some changes or corrections. Read the passage. Then read each question. Fill in the circle of the correct answer on your answer document.

(1) What is the point of education? (2) To some people, the answer is obvious: education gives you the qualifications you need to get well-paid employment, and it's a stepping stone to professional success. (3) Others believe that education should give us the tools we need to understand the world we live in. (4) It seems to me that our education system favors the former, rather than the latter. (5) The examination system in this country is designed to measure intelligence, rather than how that intelligence is applied. (6) Most national tests given to high school students in the United States are indicators of potential, rather than achievement. (7) They tell us what a student is *capable of knowing*, rather than what he or she knows already. (8) How do you measure ignorance?

(9) We should know that Earth revolves around the Sun once every twenty-four hours, but unless we're going to be physicists, how important is it to know what Einstein meant when he said that $e = mc^2$? (10) Knowing how to add, subtract, multiply, and divide makes possible the many kinds of calculations and transactions that we will make throughout our lives, but does differential calculus really make our lives happier or more meaningful? (11) So many people in the world speak English, I don't see a reason to learn any other languages. (12) Since I'm not Hamlet, the Prince of Denmark, "To be or not to be" is not a question I'll ever have to answer. (13) It seems to me that we must first of all decide what is worth knowing, and then we need to get to work learning it, testing our knowledge, and applying it to the world we live in.

15 What kind of passage is this?

A interpretive response to literature
B argumentative essay
C personal narrative
D expository article

16 Which sentence is not relevant and should be removed from the passage?

F It seems to me that our education system favors the former, rather than the latter.

G Most national tests given to high school students in the United States are indicators of potential, rather than achievement.

H How do you measure ignorance?

J Since I'm not Hamlet, the Prince of Denmark, "To be or not to be" is not a question I'll ever have to answer.

17 Which sentence could best be inserted before sentence 9 to help make the transition to the ideas in the second paragraph?

  A Knowledge of the world is as mysterious as the universe itself.

  B What subjects don't we need to know when we leave high school?

  C There are more things in heaven and Earth than can reasonably be fitted into a high school curriculum.

  D Realistically, what should we be expected to know by the time we leave high school?

18 Which would be the best word or phrase to insert at the beginning of sentence 5 to link it to sentence 4?

  F In particular,

  G To be sure,

  H Nevertheless,

  J However,

19 Which of these is a run-on sentence that should be revised?

  A sentence 3

  B sentence 7

  C sentence 11

  D sentence 12

20 What concluding sentence could best be added after sentence 13?

  F These are the sort of questions we must address if education is going to have any relevance to the real lives of real people, living in the real world.

  G We have been dodging the bullet for much too long, and we must act now before disaster strikes.

  H Then maybe we will start to come to grips with the question I asked at the top of the essay.

  J Until those decisions are made, we might as well pack up our books and go home.

GO ON

Part 2: Correcting Sentence Errors

> **Questions 21–26:** Read each sentence. One of the underlined parts may be an error in grammar or usage. Decide which underlined part, if any, should be corrected. Fill in the circle of the correct answer on your answer document.

21 The coach always told us that it didn't hardly
               A   **B**

matter whether we won or lost, so long as
C

we did the best we could, but we never
          D

believed him. Make no change.
          E

22 The reason being for the dry, settled
        F

weather was the presence of a massive
          G

concentration of high pressure over the
               H

Central Plains area, and there was no wind

to move it. Make no change.
J   **K**

23 It's so silent here in the darkened auditorium
                A

that you'd never guess there are 5,000
      B   **C**

people holding their breath and waiting for
       D

the lights to come up. Make no change.
            E

24 We waited a long time for the weather
        F

to break, and when the rain finally came, the
G   **H**

storm was incredible ferocious.
         J

Make no change.
K

25 The notorious outlaw swore that he would
      A   **B**

never come back to trouble the town again;
      C   **D**

remarkably, he never did. Make no change.
               E

26 Two of Mariel's sisters got married in
          F   **G**

September, and now she has two new

brother-in-laws named Francis and Mateo.
      H   **J**

Make no change.
K

GO ON

Questions 27–32: Read the passage. Choose the best way to write each underlined part. Fill in the circle of the correct answer on your answer document.

I have always made it a rule to buy shoes that are at least a size too small,

to <u>insure</u> that they would fit properly. Well, when I say "always," I really mean
    27

since my feet stopped <u>growing?</u> While they were still growing, I would usually
        28

buy shoes that were a size too big so my feet would grow into them. Well,

when I say "I would usually buy shoes," what I really mean is my dad would

buy them. Anyway, my point is that I buy small shoes because they expand as

you wear <u>them. At least</u>, if they're made of leather, they do.
      29

A few weeks ago, I bought a pair of boots. As you can probably

<u>guess,</u> I bought them so small that I could hardly squeeze my feet into them.
  30

They were so <u>uncomfortible</u>, I could hardly wear them for more than a half-
        31

hour at a time as I was trying to break them in. If I wore them for any longer

than that, my feet would break out in blisters. After five weeks of agony, I

limped back to the store and demanded my money back. Imagine my horror

when the assistant turned them over and displayed the soles: *100% Pure*

Omniglom. <u>Weren't leather at all!</u>
      32

27 A assure
   B ensure
   C measure
   D Make no change

28 F growing!
   G growing;
   H growing.
   J Make no change

29 A them: At least
   B them, at least
   C them—at least
   D Make no change

30 F guess;
   G guess—
   H guess
   J Make no change

31 A uncomfortable
   B uncomfertable
   C unconfortable
   D Make no change

32 F Weren't at all leather!
   G They weren't leather at all!
   H Leather at all, they weren't!
   J Make no change

GO ON

Part 3: Writing   Expository

READ

Imagine that your parents are planning to move your family from the city or town where you live to the country. Or, if you live in a rural area, imagine that your family is moving to a city or suburb. You may strongly object to the move, or you might think it's a great idea.

THINK

Think about the differences between living in a city or suburb and living in the country. What are some of the advantages and disadvantages of each experience?

WRITE

Write an essay in which you briefly compare and contrast the experiences of country versus city life.

As you write your composition, remember to —

☐ include a thesis statement that introduces the comparison and contrast between living in the country and living in the city

☐ organize your ideas in a logical order, and connect those ideas using transitions

☐ develop your ideas fully and thoughtfully with well-chosen details and observations

☐ make sure your composition is no longer than one page

Post-test

Part 1: Improving Sentences and Paragraphs

Questions 1–6: Read each sentence. Choose the best way to write the underlined part of the sentence. Fill in the circle of the correct answer on your answer document.

1 Aretha Franklin, one of America's greatest singers, <u>were inducted</u> into the Rock and Roll Hall of Fame in 1987.

  A is inducted
  B was inducted
  C being inducted
  D Make no change

2 As a child, Aretha Franklin joined the congregation of Detroit's New Bethel Baptist Church, <u>who was famous</u> for gospel singing.

  F which was famous
  G who were famous
  H that were famous
  J Make no change

3 <u>Aretha made her first recording as a fourteen-year-old gospel singer, and then she signed with Columbia Records after meeting with the legendary producer, John Hammond.</u>

  A At age fourteen Aretha made her first gospel recordings, and soon after that she met with legendary producer John Hammond, and then she signed with Columbia Records.
  B Aretha made her first recordings as a gospel singer at the age of fourteen, after a meeting with John Hammond, the legendary producer, she signed with Columbia Records.
  C Having made her first gospel recordings at fourteen, Aretha met with legendary producer John Hammond, after which she signed with Columbia Records.
  D Make no change

4 Aretha had some minor hits with Columbia in the 1960s, but songs like *Rock-a-bye Your Baby with a Dixie Melody* had not explored the full scope and depth of her talents.

    F were not exploring

    G have not explored

    H did not explore

    J Make no change

5 In 1967, Jerry Wexler, a producer for Atlantic Records, took Aretha under his wing and, most significant, introduced her to the southern rhythm-and-blues musicians at Muscle Shoals studio in Alabama.

    A mostly significant

    B most significantly

    C mostly significantly

    D Make no change

6 In collaboration with Wexler and the Muscle Shoals rhythm section, Aretha's characteristic sound was developed, which was a blend of gospel, urban rhythm-and-blues, and hard-driving rock and roll.

    F Aretha's characteristic sound, as a blend of gospel, urban rhythm-and-blues, and hard-driving rock and roll, was developed in collaboration with Wexler and the Muscle Shoals rhythm section.

    G In collaboration with Wexler and the Muscle Shoals rhythm section, a blend of gospel, urban, rhythm-and-blues, and hard-driving rock and roll was developed as Aretha's characteristic sound.

    H In collaboration with Wexler and the Muscle Shoals rhythm section, Aretha developed her characteristic sound, which was a blend of gospel, urban rhythm-and-blues, and hard driving rock and roll.

    J Make no change

Name _____ Date _____

Questions 7–8: Read each question and fill in the circle of the correct answer on your answer document.

7 Which is a complete sentence written correctly?

   A Aretha Franklin is one of the great figures of soul music, and due to the power of her voice and her sheer emotional conviction.

   B Aretha's father, a minister of the New Bethel Baptist Church in Detroit, where Aretha first encountered gospel and sang as a child in the congregation.

   C Aretha, who guards her private life very carefully and rarely grants interviews, has won eighteen Grammy awards and appeared in many movies and documentaries.

   D Aretha, winning numerous awards and great acclaim as the first woman to be inducted into the Rock and Roll Hall of Fame in 1987.

8 Which is the best way to combine these two sentences?

Aretha Franklin is the "Queen of Soul," and one of the great figures of American music.
Aretha Franklin's stature was recognized in 2005 when she was awarded the Presidential Medal of Freedom.

   F Aretha Franklin, the "Queen of Soul" and one of the great figures of American music, had her stature recognized by the Presidential Medal of Freedom in 2005.

   G Aretha Franklin's stature as the "Queen of Soul" and one of the great figures of American music was recognized in 2005 when she was awarded the Presidential Medal of Freedom.

   H Aretha Franklin was awarded the Presidential Medal of Freedom in 2005, when her stature as the "Queen of Soul" and one of the great figures of American music was recognized.

   J Aretha Franklin was recognized in 2005, when her stature as the "Queen of Soul" and one of the great figures of American music was awarded the Presidential Medal of Freedom.

Questions 9–14 refer to the following passage. Read the passage. Then read each question. Fill in the circle of the correct answer on your answer document.

(1) Thomas Paine was born the son of a corset maker in Thetford, England, in 1737. (2) An unpromising youth, Paine flunked out of school at the age of twelve and caused his father more disappointment when he quit his apprenticeship in corset making. (3) At the age of nineteen, he went to sea as a merchant sailor but disliked life aboard ship and was constantly seasick. (4) He came ashore in 1759, set up shop as a corset maker in the southern coastal town of Sandwich, got married, and tried to settle down. (5) In 1760, Paine's wife died and, shortly afterward, his business failed.

(6) He returned to Thetford and spent five unhappy years as an excise officer. (7) After signing off goods that he had failed to inspect, he was fired in 1766. (8) He worked as a domestic servant, made some more bad corsets, and applied to become a minister before taking a teaching post in Lewes, in southern England, in 1768. (9) He took lodgings above a snuff shop on High Street. (10) In 1772, Paine wrote and published his first political pamphlet, *The Case of the Officers of Excise*, which questioned the taxation system and called for better pay for excise men.

(11) In September 1774, Paine met Benjamin Franklin on a visit to London. (12) Franklin took to him and advised him to go to America. (13) Franklin wrote him letters of recommendation, and in a few weeks Paine was on his way across the Atlantic. (14) Could the shiftless Paine have had any idea, when he stepped ashore in Philadelphia on November 30, 1774, that he would soon be one of the most famous men in the western world?

9 Which sentence is not relevant to the writer's argument and should be removed?

A At the age of nineteen, he went to sea as a merchant sailor but disliked life aboard ship and was constantly seasick.

B In 1760, Paine's wife died and, shortly afterward, his business failed.

C He took lodgings above a snuff shop on High Street.

D Franklin wrote him letters of recommendation, and in a few weeks Paine was on his way across the Atlantic.

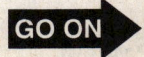
GO ON

10 Which is the best way to join the two underlined sentences (11 and 12) to make a single sentence?

F On a visit to London in September 1774, Paine met Benjamin Franklin, who took to him and advised him to go to America.

G In September 1774, Paine met Benjamin Franklin on a visit to London, who took to him and advised him to go to America

H On a visit to London in September 1774, Paine met Benjamin Franklin, who advised him and took him to America.

J Paine met Benjamin Franklin, who took him on a visit to London in September 1774, and advised him to go to America.

11 Which sentence from the passage is a complex sentence?

A sentence 4

B sentence 5

C sentence 6

D sentence 7

12 Which is the best sentence to insert before sentence 1 to make the passage more appealing to readers?

F One writer, whose *Common Sense* fired the American Revolutionary War and whose *Rights of Man* inspired the French Revolution, grew up poor.

G In early America, all of the Founding Fathers were accomplished writers, and much of what they wrote can still be read today.

H Heroes come in many strange shapes and forms, and few are stranger than the failed corset maker who inspired two continents to revolution.

J As Shakespeare wrote, "Some men are born great, some achieve greatness, and some have greatness thrust upon them."

13 Which of these would be the best sentence to insert before sentence 6 to introduce the second paragraph?

A Things went from bad to worse.

B At the age of twenty three, Thomas Paine was jobless and aimless.

C But there were more important things in life than corsets.

D The future author of *Common Sense* and *The Rights of Man* was a mess at this time.

14 Which sentence should be added after sentence 14 to conclude this piece?

F Could he have foreseen the sad end that also awaited him, after the years of struggle and glory?

G Twelve years after his arrival, Paine invented an ingenious iron bridge.

H Truth is sometimes stranger than fiction, and Thomas Paine was a good example of this.

J Perhaps more than any other writer of his time, Thomas Paine helped to incite revolution in America and change the course of history.

Questions 15–20: A student wrote this passage. It may need some changes or corrections. Read the passage. Then read each question. Fill in the circle of the correct answer on your answer document.

(1) To what degree can animals understand what we are saying? (2) Many stories I've read have examples of dogs, cats, and other creatures who can comprehend and even master human speech. (3) The medieval hero, Renaud de Montauban, rode a bay horse called Bayard, who understood every word his rider spoke. (4) The English writer Saki wrote a famous short story in which a cat called Tobermory is taught human language and uses his talents to embarrass the guests at a country house by repeating their private indiscretions in public. (5) Animal languages remain largely mysterious—at least, to humans. (6) In literature, talking animals belong to the realm of fantasy. (7) In real life, however, we are often amazed at how much animals seem to understand.

(8) Recently, my friend Cal and I went down to the ocean to swim. (9) Cal had his Welsh sheepdog Wendy with him. (10) We crossed the boardwalk, climbed over the railing, and jumped down about six feet onto the sand. (11) Wendy hung back; the jump was too high for her. (12) Cal said, "You need to come down by the steps, Wendy." (13) He hardly even gestured toward the steps, which must have been 200 yards away. (14) Wendy sped off, and a minute later she joined us on the sand. (15) Wendy had never been to that beach before.

(16) I asked Cal how she understood to come around by the steps. (17) He seemed surprised by my question. (18) "Because I told her to," he said.

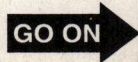

15 What type of passage is this?

A interpretive response to literature
B informative article
C argumentative essay
D reflective narrative

16 What pattern of organization does the writer use to organize this passage?

F thesis with supporting examples
G problem and solution
H comparison and contrast
J chronological order

17 Which would be the best sentence to insert before sentence 8 to help make the transition to the ideas in the next paragraph?

A Here's what I'm talking about, in case you don't believe me.
B Dog owners take this kind of thing for granted.
C Dogs are probably more attentive to human speech than cats.
D Of all the animals, dogs are the most intelligent.

18 Which sentence is inappropriate and should be removed from this passage?

F Many stories I've read have examples of dogs, cats, and other creatures who can comprehend and even master human speech.
G Animal languages remain largely mysterious—at least, to humans.
H In literature, talking animals belong to the realm of fantasy.
J He hardly even gestured toward the steps, which must have been 200 yards away.

19 Which would be the best clause or phrase to insert into sentence 14 to link it to sentence 13?

A Like a meter,
B Although I have no proof,
C To my amazement,
D If you can believe it,

20 If this passage continued, what information would be most logical to add in the next paragraph of the passage?

F more examples of how animals understand human speech
G a brief discussion of how whales and dolphins communicate with one another
H a scientific analysis of the way human brain functions differ from those of various animals
J further discussion of the way dog owners speak to their animals

Part 2: Correcting Sentence Errors

Name _____ Date _____

> **Questions 21–26:** Read each sentence. One of the underlined parts may be an error in grammar or usage. Decide which underlined part, if any, should be corrected. Fill in the circle of the correct answer on your answer document.

21 When *Bad Day at Sagebrush* was cast, I
A
was disappointed to be given the part of
B
Concerned Townsman, who comes on in
C
Act Two and says, "It's going to be a long,
D
hot summer." Make no change.
E

22 The principal gave Jack and me the benefit
F
of the doubt, because she clearly believed
there were others who were more
G
responsible for what happened than
H
Jack or I. Make no change.
J   **K**

23 We could ve gotten the work finished much
A
earlier if Tanya and Lily had arrived on time
B   **C**
instead of two hours late. Make no change.
D   **E**

24 Although we didn't have to go to the
F
basketball game, we decided we would go,
if only because none of us couldn't think of
G   **H**
any good reason not to go. Make no change.
J   **K**

25 Even though we had not booked anywhere
A   **B**
to stay, the village was deserted when we
arrived, and we had no difficulty finding
C
inexpensive and comfortable
accomodations. Make no change.
D   **E**

26 After days of waiting in the bitter cold, they
at last heard the sound of artillery fire,
F
muffled by the dense forest and the heavy
G
snow; Napoleon's army had broken through
H   **J**
their lines. Make no change.
K

GO ON ➤

> **Questions 27–32:** Read the passage. Choose the best way to write each underlined part. Fill in the circle of the correct answer on your answer document.

Members of the mainstream media are very concerned about the

increasing popularity and influence of blogs. The word "blog" is a shortened

form of <u>"web log" which originally</u> referred to the personal journals that people
27

began to post on the Internet in the <u>1990's.</u> The Internet is not subject to the
28

same restraints as the <u>mainstream media</u>, and these early blogs were often
29

highly opinionated and mischievous. Readers could post comments <u>direct</u> on
30

to the bloggers' websites, generating "threads" of <u>discussion . . . in</u> this way,
31

readers became bloggers themselves. In recent years, blogs have evolved into

large interactive sites, dealing with a vast range of topics. Many blogs cover

politics and current affairs. More and more people are going to blogs for their

news, in <u>preference</u> to newspapers and TV. The mainstream media have tried
32

to counter the threat by reporting what is being said in the "Blogosphere" and

by giving bloggers airtime on TV and radio.

27 **A** "web log," which originally

   B "web log"—which originally

   C "web log;" which originally

   D Make no change

28 **F** 1990ies

   G 1990s

   H 1990s'

   J Make no change

29 **A** Mainstream media

   B mainstream Media

   C Mainstream Media

   D Make no change

30 **F** directed

   G directly

   H directing

   J Make no change

31 **A** discussion—in

   B discussion: in

   C discussion-in

   D Make no change

32 **F** reference

   G deference

   H conference

   J Make no change

GO ON

Part 3: Writing   Persuasive

READ

Scientists estimate that as many as a hundred animal species become extinct every day! The situation is so critical for some species that their only chance for survival is to live in zoos and wildlife refuges.

THINK

Think about the critical situation facing many animal species. Is it right to preserve species in artificial or managed environments, or should we allow them to become extinct when their natural habitats are lost or destroyed?

WRITE

Write an argumentative essay in which you clearly state and defend a position on the issue of preserving species in artificial environments. Give reasons and examples to support your views.

As you write your composition, remember to —

☐ include a thesis statement that clearly states a position on the issue of preserving species in artificial environments

☐ organize your ideas in a logical order, and connect those ideas using transitions

☐ develop your ideas fully and thoughtfully with well-chosen reasons and observations

☐ make sure your composition is no longer than one page